THE *Church* GOD BLESSES

Books by Jim Cymbala

Fresh Wind, Fresh Fire
Fresh Faith
Fresh Power
God's Grace from Ground Zero
The Life God Blesses
The Church God Blesses

THE *Church* GOD BLESSES

JIM CYMBALA

PASTOR OF THE BROOKLYN TABERNACLE

with Stephen Sorenson

ZONDERVAN™

GRAND RAPIDS, MICHIGAN 49530

ZONDERVAN™

The Church God Blesses
Copyright © 2002 by Jim Cymbala

Requests for information should be addressed to:
Zondervan, *Grand Rapids, Michigan 49530*

Library of Congress Cataloging-in-Publication Data
Cymbala, Jim, 1943-
  The church God blesses / Jim Cymbala, with Stephen Sorenson.
    p. cm.
  ISBN 0-310-24203-7
1. Church. I. Sorenson, Stephen. II. Title.
BV600.3.C95 2002
262'.0017'7—dc21   2001007126

This edition printed on acid-free paper.

The story of Jay Tucker in chapter 5 is adapted with permission from the archives of the Assemblies of God World Missions Department.

Published in association with the literary agency of Ann Spangler & Associates, 1420 Pontiac Road SE, Grand Rapids, MI 49506.

Interior design by Melissa Elenbaas

Printed in the United States of America

02 03 04 05 06 07 08 09 /❖ WZ/ 10 9 8 7 6 5 4 3 2 1

CONTENTS

PROLOGUE

SOMETHING BETTER

Every advancement in the way people live has come about because someone saw what could be and was no longer willing to accept what is. This is true of virtually all the inventions that have impacted human civilization. The men and women responsible for those breakthroughs imagined something that was not yet visible to the human eye. Not all of these people were geniuses, but they all had vision. They refused to yield to the idea that there was no better way to do things and pressed on toward something better, even though the process often required years of hard work and many failures along the

way. Consequently, countless people in succeed-
ing generations have reaped the benefits.

The starting point for this advancement was
people who did not settle for the status quo but
believed that things could be different and better.
This fact is just as true in the spiritual realm.
Every revival in church history has been started
by pastors and believers who became deeply
dissatisfied with the moral and spiritual climate
around them. They knew from Scripture that God
had something better for his people. All the great
missionary movements have been spawned by
men and women who became desperate to see
God's kingdom extended to *new* regions and to
those who had not yet heard about Jesus. In fact,
every time people really pray, they are believing
that God by his divine power can change *what is*
into *something better*.

The Bible is full of declarations about God's
desire to bring about dramatic change when his
children are missing out on his promised blessings.
In the Old Testament, God's ability to overcome all
obstacles and help his people is illustrated time and
time again through individuals such as Abraham,
Joseph, Moses, and David. They stand out, along

with a few others, as exceptions to the general hard-heartedness and unbelief that existed among the children of Israel.

In the New Testament, however, the focus changes to the churches of the Lord Jesus Christ and the ministers who serve within them. Starting with the birth of the church in Jerusalem (Acts 2), the gospel is preached, lives are transformed by the Holy Spirit's power, and a congregation is formed as shepherds are carefully placed over God's flock. This same spiritual sequence is repeated in city after city. Through these local churches filled with spiritually transformed people, God works further change in ever-widening circles throughout the world. The book of Acts recounts these wonderful stories as the Lord's message and power spread throughout the Roman Empire.

Even though individual lives are being changed by the power of the gospel, God's special concern is always focused on the local churches that spread his gospel and disciple new converts. In fact, the New Testament is composed mostly of letters sent to these local assemblies or to the ministers who exercised spiritual leadership among them. Jesus himself wrote seven letters to different local congregations (Revelation 2–3) and was seen walking among *them* as their resurrected Lord (Revelation 1:13). It is evident that nothing is more important to the Lord than the spiritual state of the local churches that bear his name.

Heaven's great concern is not for the United Nations, global warming, or the financial markets of the world. Heaven's great concern is for the extension of God's kingdom, the spreading of the gospel, the world coming to understand who he really is—and all of this depends on local Christian churches like yours and mine. God is not using angels to represent himself, nor will a voice be heard from heaven to preach the gospel. He has chosen to work here on earth through his church.

Obviously, not all Christian churches are in a healthy spiritual condition, and therein lies a great problem. Some churches are worldly, mere infants in Christ that are not ready for solid spiritual food (1 Corinthians 3:1–2). Others are susceptible to a false gospel, which is no gospel at all (Galatians 1:6–7). Some congregations have been placed in hostile spiritual territory—even "where Satan has his throne"—yet they remain true to Christ

(Revelation 2:13). Others have lost their first love of Christ and need to repent quickly (Revelation 2:4–5). Some stand as models to believers everywhere because of their strong faith in God (1 Thessalonians 1:7–8). Still others are so complacent and lukewarm that Jesus is about to spit them out of his mouth (Revelation 3:16–17).

But the Bible is always reminding us that things don't have to remain the way they are. If God is given the opportunity, his blessings can bring about dramatic change no matter what our circumstances are. No negative situation, hostile environment, or shortage of manpower is greater than the power of Jesus Christ. He alone can transform any local congregation into something more wonderful than we could ever imagine.

Even in his letter to the church that was at risk of being vomited out of his mouth, Jesus closed by exclaiming, "Here I am! I stand at the door and knock. *If anyone hears my voice and opens the door*, I will come in and eat with him, and he with me" (Revelation 3:20). How tender and compassionate our Lord is in wanting to heal the worst of our church situations! He desires the best for our churches so that his name will be honored and the world will be affected by his message going out through strong and vibrant believers. Who else can God use but his own church? And we alone can make the decision to "open the door" to our Lord.

We who consider ourselves serious believers in Christ have to face this obvious question: Will we settle for the status quo in our own church situations, or will we reach out for what God can supernaturally do? The Lord is eager to make spiritual changes among us and shower us with his blessings. He wants us—his people—to experience the greatness of his power and the depth of his love in a new way. All he needs from us is a listening ear and a heart that believes that with God all things are possible.

ONE

THE BABY
UNDER ATTACK

Carol and I have often read the Christmas story in Matthew 2, which includes King Herod's vicious attack on the babies of Bethlehem in his efforts to seek and destroy Jesus, the newborn King. From this story we thought we understood that Satan often attacks the "baby" when it is young and vulnerable. Through the experiences of others we had learned that when a new ministry for Christ begins or when someone steps out in faith to do God's will, Satan will often try to squelch what God is doing right at the outset—before it gathers momentum and builds a stronger faith.

As we began our ministry at the Brooklyn Tabernacle, we both thought we understood and were prepared for Satan's attacks. We were (and still are) hungry to be like the early Christians who so powerfully experienced the Lord's hand on their lives. Carol and I wanted the Brooklyn Tabernacle to be a place where God's grace would be clearly evident and not just talked about. But soon we learned just how intense it can get when the "baby" is under attack.

The story of this satanic attack actually begins with some precious verses in the New Testament that God used in a tremendous way in my life. They paint a beautiful picture of the church God blesses:

> Now those [Christians] who had been scattered by the persecution in connection with Stephen traveled as far as Phoenicia, Cyprus and Antioch, telling the message only to Jews. Some of them, however, men from Cyprus and Cyrene, went to Antioch and began to speak to Greeks also, telling them the good news about the Lord Jesus. *The Lord's hand was with them,* and a great

number of people believed and turned to
the Lord (Acts 11:19–21).

WHAT'S THE SECRET?

The great Christian church in Antioch was
begun, surprisingly, by some unknown and
unnamed "men from Cyprus and Cyrene." So
what was the real secret of its wonderful birth?
One simple phrase tells it all: "The Lord's hand
was with them." With no New Testament yet
written, surrounded by hostile Jews and
Romans, with no benefit from a legalized religion
or formal church buildings, with no apparent
source of income, with no printed materials or
sound systems or choirs or seminary training,
anonymous believers started one of the most
dynamic congregations of the Christian era.

The Bible offers no specifics concerning the
methodology or doctrinal statement of its
founders. We are told only that "the Lord's hand
was with them." Because of God's blessings, this
church evidently led multitudes of people to the
Lord Jesus Christ in repentance and faith! It

didn't matter what was *against* these believers because God's blessings and grace were *for* them in a remarkable way.

Soon the older church in Jerusalem heard about God's blessing being poured upon this unique, Jewish/Gentile congregation in Antioch. The leaders sent a trusted man, Barnabas, to confirm the wonderful reports. Acts 11:23 records what happened next: "When he arrived and *saw the evidence of the grace of God,* he was glad and encouraged them all to remain true to the Lord with all their hearts."

Barnabas "saw the evidence" that God was blessing and at work in special ways. The church in Antioch had no publicity department or magazine to sing its praises, but it needed nothing of the sort. When unbelievers are repenting of sin and turning to the Lord, when mass water baptismal services have to be scheduled, when there are strong congregational prayer meetings, when there is a spirit of unity and love among believers—that, my friends, is a little of heaven right here on earth!

The whole impact of these unnamed believers and the church they founded revolves around the fact that "the Lord's hand was with them." And what occurred in Antioch about two thousand years ago can also occur today. No matter where we are, we can experience God's blessings to the extent that his hand of power is with us. Whether we are pastors, teachers, evangelists, Christian education workers, or music ministers or have other positions in our local churches, we can all accomplish more for God's kingdom than we have ever dreamed if we learn the secret of asking the Lord to stretch out his hand and do what only he can do in our midst.

No matter where we are,

we can experience God's blessings to the

extent that his hand of power is with us.

This is God's plan for our lives as individual Christians as well as in being part of "his body, which is the church" (Colossians 1:24). Our main calling is to live in fellowship with Christ and to labor with him in extending his kingdom. To miss out on this is to forfeit the deep sense of fulfillment and joy that comes only when we are partnering with Jesus. It also means that we miss out on *life* as God intended it and exist only on a physical level that will never satisfy the yearning of our souls. Job summarized things well when he observed, "Naked I came from my mother's womb, and naked I will depart" (Job 1:21). Every home, every automobile, and all our investments will evaporate in one split second at the coming of Christ. But if we enjoy the blessings of God and labor for the cause of Christ—that has significance for both now and all eternity.

SATAN, OUR CEASELESS ADVERSARY

Satan knows all about the crucial role that local churches play in the building of God's kingdom. In fact, he has suffered much loss when congregations have properly connected with the living Christ. Because of the threat that all Christian congregations are to Satan, churches are his special target. He cleverly uses every device possible to make us ineffective.

Satan begins by attempting to deceive Christians concerning the vital importance of the local church and its potential in God. He wants them to think that "church" is only a place you visit on Sundays . . . if you can spare the time. Our adversary tries to bury some congregations under an avalanche of traditionalism and lifeless ceremony. Many churches he makes ineffective by stifling and discouraging the spirit of prayer. Elsewhere, he instigates strife and division, gossip and fighting—all of which are aimed at grieving away the Holy Spirit's presence and power. Church splits also benefit his demonic design. He tries to neutralize some churches through false doctrine, emotional fanaticism, or harsh attitudes. And, of course, pastors and other ministers come under continual and intense personal or spiritual attack because Satan knows that many believers are hurt and weakened when a leader falls.

How tragic it is that so many believers pore over daily newspapers to learn about the latest world events when the things that are *most important* to God are happening right in our own churches! Today we desperately need not only spiritual revival among our churches but an awakening to the importance that Jesus places on *every* Christian congregation. How can Christianity be more victorious than Christian churches?

The story of the church in Antioch was a turning point of sorts for Carol and me when we first entered the ministry. As a pastor I was stirred by the potential a local congregation could have through God. The handful of people who were attending the Brooklyn Tabernacle when we came there, the squalid downtown neighborhood in which the church was located, our lack of formal training and experience in the ministry—all of these factors made us yearn for some experience of "the Lord's hand" being with us. *If God could pour abundant grace upon the church in Antioch amid such hostile and limited circumstances,* we thought, *what is so impossible about our dilemma?* Together with a small group during our Tuesday night prayer meetings, Carol and I began to plead with God to pour out his grace again.

THE UNUSUAL TELEPHONE CALL

It was about that time that one particular Sunday ended with an unusual phone call about 11 P.M. The caller was a pastor in South Dakota whom we had never met. Even today I have no idea how he obtained our home phone number. He sounded passionate and earnest as he shared with me his burden for inner-city work. He said the Lord seemed to be directing his family our way and wanted to know if we could use some help. I listened politely, then spoke honestly about our situation. I explained that we were new at the church, novices in the ministry, and had no financial resources. (In fact, both of us were working second jobs just to make ends meet.) I was noncommittal about his coming to work with us because I didn't know him at all, but I promised to pray that God would direct his steps.

The next phone call from this pastor, one week later almost to the minute, was more surprising. "My wife, two kids, and I are packing up and leaving for New York tomorrow!" he said. God had supposedly spoken clearly to them, and they felt they needed to obey the call to work for Christ in the inner city.

This turn of events unnerved me a bit since I had no idea what he was expecting from us. We hadn't invited him or even encouraged him to come. Our church situation was anything but promising. But what could I say? He was driving to New York and would be arriving in a matter of days. I asked him to call me when he reached the New Jersey state line.

Four days later I received his call and gave them directions to our home. I went to the supermarket to buy some groceries for dinner and picked out the cheapest steaks that were on sale. We didn't have much money, but we wanted to be as hospitable and gracious as possible.

The pastor and his wife were as young as we were and had two beautiful children. We had a pleasant meal and listened to their plans to make their lives really count for God now that they had arrived in the Big Apple. I was too shy and inexperienced to ask about their former pastorate or how they were able to leave South Dakota on such short notice.

When the meal ended, we were faced with an obvious dilemma. They had no place to stay since this move was all about "stepping out in faith." I initially didn't have a solution, but I eventually offered them a bedroom on the second floor of the church. It wasn't much, but an elderly lady lived up there in a tiny apartment and another church member lived on the premises with her daughter. The pastor and his family could share kitchen and bathroom facilities with either family for a while. But for how long, and where was this all going? They left our home and proceeded to the church, where we agreed we would see them again on Sunday.

Friday night activities at the church the next day gave our visitors a chance to meet a few members of our tiny congregation. The pastor and his wife sat together on Sunday morning, and during the evening service I introduced them. We chatted afterward, and I noticed he had gotten friendly with some of the members very quickly. Everything was going along fine, or so it seemed.

The first hint of trouble came the next day when I received a call from the woman who lived in the church with her daughter. She was very loyal to my wife and me, and that was the reason she was calling. "You have a real problem on your hands," she said, "and it happens to be that visiting pastor and his wife." She had overheard them criticizing us to some church folks and saying that we were living high on the hog while not caring about the congregation's needs.

According to her, they even criticized us for regularly eating expensive steaks!

I found what she said unbelievable. The couple seemed so nice and hadn't been in New York City for even a week. I told her to relax and not to worry, thinking that she must have misunderstood what they had said.

That night I began to study and pray about the next day, which involved a full day at the church and also conducting our Tuesday night service. Suddenly a tremendous spirit of prayer began to grip my soul. The Holy Spirit seemed to intercede in and through me as I poured out my heart to God. Hours went by as I continued to seek the Lord with tears and a strong crying out to him. The odd thing is that it seemed my great burden was for me and not someone else.

The odd thing is that it seemed my great burden was for me and not someone else.

I knelt, I sat, and I paced around the house with no seeming relief from this strong desire to pray. It was now past midnight, but still all my spiritual senses were being exercised in a very unusual way. Finally, about 2 A.M. I began to think about my need for getting some rest for the next day.

SPIRITUAL ATTACK!

I arrived at the church about 9:30 A.M. and went to the kitchen, where I usually had some coffee. The minister and his wife joined me a littler later, and we sat together at the table. I wanted to get that woman's phone call off my mind before the day went on much further, so I related to them the report I had received about their conversations with others. Was it true what she reported to me? If so, why would they say such false and hurtful things?

The pastor and his wife looked at each other for a moment, then he spoke. "Maybe we should tell him now, honey. What do you think?"

She looked up in a weird kind of way and began to laugh very slowly and in very low tones. "Yes, tell him now! It's time."

He stood up quickly and whirled at me. "You're through here, Jim. It's all over for you and your wife. You'll never preach here again. God has sent us to take over and get things right!" Then they both started grinning and laughing in those low-pitched tones.

At that point I sat in my chair bewildered and numb. *Who are these people, and what exactly is going on in this kitchen?* But they weren't done—not by a long shot. Both of them stood up and began circling me—talking, accusing, and boasting, but all of it within a spiritual framework. Their personal attack was an assault like nothing I had ever encountered before. They proceeded to enumerate all the reasons why I had to leave and claimed that God had clearly spoken to them.

I tried very hard to reason with them, but my efforts escalated things into a full-blown verbal battle that went on for hours. We went from room to room, and their intensity was incredible. A few times I felt weakened in my resolve and wondered if I should just walk away and yield to them. Their tenacity and accusations would wear me down. But then something within my heart would stir me up to withstand them again.

The couple told me the names of church members who "agreed with them" and wanted me out and them placed in charge. The eighty-year-old woman who lived in the church supposedly supported them. She had loaned the Brooklyn Tabernacle fifteen thousand dollars when a previous pastor had purchased the building, and the couple informed me that if they didn't take over she'd demand that the loan be paid in full immediately! That thought totally flabbergasted me, so I immediately knocked on her apartment door. To my shock, they had in fact turned her against me. She sided with their argument that "your time is up."

I was stunned. *How could this couple have done all this mischief in less than a week? What evil power am I dealing with, anyway?* As I stood next to that elderly woman, I turned and saw both of them near the door grinning at me with a kind of devilish glee. In an instant my lack of experience, naïveté, and desire to reason with them evaporated. For the first time I clearly saw what I was up against. And it produced one short statement from me as I stared at the man who had seemed so sincere and innocent. "You devil!" I yelled.

Suddenly the man let out a horrible, loud cry and started running toward me at full speed. I had an instant to react, but I just closed my eyes and stood still. He stopped less than a foot from me, and to this day I'm so glad that the Lord was watching over me and that the man didn't hit me. (If he had punched me and my fleshly instincts had taken over, I probably would have thrown him out of the second-floor window.)

My next words shocked me. "You and your family are leaving right now, or I am calling the police." Tears filled my eyes. We had been arguing back and forth for more than four hours, and I was like a tired fighter who had reached the end of a grueling bout.

The couple didn't seem weary at all. In fact, they suddenly changed tactics and pleaded with me to let them stay. They now told me that they deeply admired me and that it would be a privilege to work by my side!

This sudden turn left me totally confused, but I remained firm. "No," I said, "you *have* to go." Something inside me kept warning me not to yield to their pleas for "just one more night's stay." I felt there would be nothing left of our little church if they stayed on the premises.

Forcing this couple to leave was a hard, emotionally draining decision for me. It took another hour for my decision to sink into their heads. I even had to help them carry out all their boxes as they loaded up their car. Finally, about 4:30 P.M. they drove away from our rundown little building.

No words can express the spiritual, mental, and emotional fatigue I felt. I was young then, and full of energy, but during the next week all I could do was lie on our living room sofa every day for hours on end. Carol knew the gist of what had happened, but no one could possibly understand the intensity of this satanic attack. No wonder God had kept me up most of an entire night in fervent prayer! He had supernaturally prepared me for an intense battle so that I could be "strong in the Lord and in his mighty power" and able to "stand against the devil's schemes" (Ephesians 6:10–11).

RENEWED HOPE

As I recovered from this exhausting incident, key questions remained. Why did Satan make such a determined assault on a tiny church that had so many problems? Why had he tried to drive away an inexperienced, fumbling young pastor and his equally untrained wife? I pondered questions such as these as I waited before the Lord in prayer.

The devil had definitely attacked our struggling church while it was quite vulnerable, but why? Did God have something wonderful in store for us? Did God's plans incite Satan's malicious assault? I know that Satan is limited in his knowledge, but is it possible that he saw something developing in our outwardly pathetic situation that instigated his attack? Perhaps he had an inkling that soon dozens, then hundreds, and today almost two thousand people would gather every Tuesday night to pray and intercede in Jesus' name for men and women held captive to sin and Satan. Maybe he knew that former drug addicts, lawyers, former homosexuals, doctors, blacks, whites, Latinos, and Asians would one day lift up their voices together to praise God for transforming their lives. Maybe he knew that one day my untrained, shy wife would stand before 275 Brooklyn Tabernacle Choir members and proclaim to the world through song that "the Lamb has overcome."

As I pondered the possibilities, my spiritual trauma and fatigue slowly changed into fresh hope that God, in fact, had something beautiful in store for our ministry and the Brooklyn

Tabernacle. What Satan meant for evil, God in the end worked out for our good (Genesis 50:20).

What Satan meant for evil, God in the end worked out for our good.

This is a very important truth for every ministry and church that serves the Lord Jesus Christ. Whenever people stir themselves to seek the Lord, whenever someone steps out in faith upon God's promises, whenever a fresh consecration is made to yield oneself completely to him—that is the very time when Satan's most cunning attacks will often occur. We must never be surprised or alarmed when the baby comes under attack and Satan tries to snuff out the fresh, new thing God is preparing to do.

THE ATTACK ON YOUNG JOSEPH

Do you remember the moving story of Joseph in the Old Testament? Here was a case when tremendous difficulty came right after a significant blessing from God. Young Joseph had dreams indicating that God would promote him to a future position of leadership and authority. (Joseph had not asked for these dreams but believed they were of divine origin.) You might think that his family rejoiced because God's special favor rested on one of their own. It was just the opposite. Joseph's brothers, who didn't like him anyway, now "hated him all the more" (Genesis 37:5). Even Jacob, his father, rebuked him and felt he was getting too big for his britches.

But God was getting ready to use Joseph's life to accomplish his plan for an entire nation. Instead of discerning any of this, his brothers nearly killed him and ended up selling him down the river as a slave to Midianite merchants.

As Joseph traveled south in that caravan heading toward what seemed like oblivion, what must have been his thoughts concerning those prophetic dreams from God? How could they ever be fulfilled now that the bottom had fallen out of his life? As usual, Satan had attempted at the outset to foil the purposes of God. But the very hatred and jealousy Satan stirred up in order to destroy Joseph helped to fulfill the very dreams God had given the young man!

In Egypt, after many more trials, Joseph ended up being promoted to second in command of the entire nation. All of this happened because "the LORD was with Joseph" (Genesis 39:2). God did far more than Joseph could have imagined despite the devil's attacks when he was young and vulnerable. And so it is for every ministry and church that clings to the promises of God's blessing and protection.

If God is for us, who *can* be against us? God's plan to use us for his glory cannot be thwarted by any weapon formed against us. Opposition, jealousy, and hatred should never cause us to become discouraged. Rather, these things ought to cause us to rejoice that God is up to something great! Why else would Satan go to such lengths to discourage us and tempt us to look away from God's sure promises?

Don't quit believing today in what God has made real to your heart. No matter how unlikely or even hopeless the situation seems to be, God is able to fulfill his word concerning your life, your ministry, and your church.

AN IMPORTANT REMINDER

Finally, remember that when Moses was sent by God to confront Pharaoh concerning the Hebrew

slaves, his "ministry" did not get off to a spec-
tacular start. Satan, as always, was there trying to
nip things in the bud. It took tremendous courage
for Moses to approach the ruler of mighty Egypt
and demand that God's people be allowed to worship Jehovah in the desert. Despite his fears,
Moses obeyed and delivered the word of the Lord
to Pharaoh. The result? Pharaoh dismissed him as
a nuisance and a troublemaker who was distracting the Hebrews from their work. And then
Pharaoh gave new orders:

> "You are no longer to supply the people
> with straw for making bricks; let them
> go and gather their own straw. But
> require them to make the same number
> of bricks as before; don't reduce the
> quota. They are lazy; that is why they
> are crying out, 'Let us go and sacrifice to
> our God.' Make the work harder for the
> men so that they keep working and pay
> no attention to lies" (Exodus 5:7–9).

Instead of delivering God's people from
bondage, Moses got them into hot water with
Pharaoh and caused tremendous new hardships.

The Israelite foremen were so angered by the mess Moses had seemingly caused that they accused him of having "made us a stench to Pharaoh and his officials" and of putting "a sword in their hand to kill us" (Exodus 5:21).

Think of the many times Satan has used this strategy against God's servants and his church. In the very act of stepping out in faith to obey the clear calling of God, turmoil, opposition, and seeming chaos are the only visible results. All of hell works in concert to keep us from pursuing what God has shown us. Every obstacle imaginable is put in our way in order to cause fear, discouragement, and then finally to make us give up.

But the people blessed by God must persevere no matter what. They must understand that Satan fights the hardest when the greatest spiritual breakthroughs and blessings are just around the corner. Yet, even as the Christ child in Bethlehem was rescued from what seemed to be certain doom, so also God will protect and nurture his chosen people.

God has begun a good work in us, and he will bring it to completion as we wait in faith (Philippians 1:6). Then we will join in singing

the song of another of God's blessed servants
who experienced the attacks of the enemy:

> The Lord is my light and my salvation—
>   whom shall I fear?
> The Lord is the stronghold of my life—
>   of whom shall I be afraid?
> When evil men advance against me
>   to devour my flesh,
> when my enemies and my foes attack me,
>   they will stumble and fall.
> Though an army besiege me,
>   my heart will not fear;
> though war break out against me,
>   even then will I be confident. . . .
> I am still confident of this:
>   I will see the goodness of the Lord
>   in the land of the living.
> Wait for the Lord;
>   be strong and take heart
>   and wait for the Lord (Psalm 27:1–3,
>   13–14).

*Father, help us to trust you no matter what
we see with our natural eyes. Take away our
discouragement and fear so we can serve you*

with boldness. Stretch out your hand, as you have in the past, so we can experience your supernatural grace in new ways. We will be careful to give Jesus Christ all the honor and praise due his name. Amen.

TWO

OUR SPIRITUAL DIET

People might not be thinking much about the eternal destiny of their souls nowadays, but they sure are getting better educated about their physical bodies on earth. Diet and nutrition are two of the hottest topics around and the source of billion-dollar industries. Those who are "in the know" focus on much more than just length of life and disease prevention. They maintain that energy levels, emotional stability, and even clarity of thought can be dramatically affected by what we eat. More and more of us are becoming convinced of how important the chemical balance within our bodies is. We are getting new insights into the saying, "You are what you eat." What we take into our bodies does affect how we feel, think, and live.

I am certainly no expert on this subject, but a woman's recent experience gave me a new perspective on this whole matter. Maria, the wife of a pastor-friend of mine, had been struggling with her health for quite a while. We had often prayed for her during our staff meetings at the Brooklyn Tabernacle, so I asked my friend a few months ago how she was doing. That's when I heard her amazing story.

AN EXPERIMENT THAT WORKED

Maria's physical problems began more than nine years ago with pulmonary disease and a developing asthmatic condition. The past three years proved to be really hard on her. The increased use of antibiotics, steroids of all sorts, a nebulizer, and four different kinds of pumps had taken a toll. Maria was a very sick lady. The heavy doses of medication led to phlebitis in her legs. She also contracted pneumonia three times within four years. Her sinuses became so impacted that doctors recommended surgery—and it would not be a simple one. There would be a long, painful recovery because of the sensitive area involved.

Just one week before the scheduled surgery, Maria contacted a nutritionist. Convinced that the surgery would be treating the manifestation of her problem, not its root cause, he examined her carefully and recommended a specialized diet that supposedly would improve her condition. Her husband was very skeptical and sure that surgery was unavoidable. *How could a change in diet,* he wondered, *correct nine years of chronic physical problems that have grown so serious?*

Maria kept to the diet and after a few days canceled the surgery. One week later she was no longer gasping for air. She needed no pumps, no nebulizer, and no more antibiotics. Her husband was so amazed by her total turnaround that he made an appointment to see the nutritionist himself! Today his wife feels great and is full of energy.

Obviously, not all medical conditions can be improved or so quickly remedied by a change of diet. But no matter how we feel about the negatives of fats and carbohydrates and the pluses of fruits and vegetables, we can't deny that our bodies operate according to physical laws. Nor can we deny that the consequences of these laws are inescapable. Health problems, energy levels, and mood swings *are* often related to diet. (I had a friend in college whose personality was visibly altered every time he ate two or three Snickers bars!)

NURTURING OUR SPIRITUAL BEING

However, we need more than merely a balanced diet to be totally healthy. Even though we are complex physical beings, we are more essentially and importantly spiritual beings! This is what separates us from the animal kingdom that has no spiritual nature. And just as vibrant health and growth in the physical realm are critically dependent on a proper, well-balanced diet, so also our spiritual side is in critical need of proper spiritual food. That is why God spoke these words through the prophet Isaiah:

> "Come, all you who are thirsty,
>   come to the waters;
> and you who have no money,
>   come, buy and eat!

Come, buy wine and milk
    without money and without cost.
Why spend money on what is not bread,
    and your labor on what does not
        satisfy?
Listen, listen to me, and eat what is
        good,
    and your soul will delight in the
        richest of fare" (Isaiah 55:1–2).

Although there is the general theme in Scripture that only salvation through Jesus Christ satisfies the spiritual longing we all have, there is a more specific application of the reference to "water," "wine," "milk," and "bread" in this passage. These words refer to an important spiritual principle from which no one is exempt. Just as physical problems result from improper diet and vitamin deficiencies, *spiritual* problems often result when we are spiritually undernourished. Even as diabetes, high cholesterol, and a host of other problems can be treated by a change of diet, so numerous things can be accomplished in our lives as Christians when we follow a simple but radical change of diet. "You are what you eat" is all too true in the spiritual realm, but many believers are living in a state of denial about the real cause of their problems.

———————— ✦ ————————

You are what you eat" is all too true in the spiritual realm, but many believers are living in a state of denial about the real cause of their problems.

It is very possible to be a Christian who is born again in the scriptural sense, but at the same time be ill and weak due to spiritual malnutrition. This explains so much about the joyless, semidepressed, and unfruitful living among many believers today. I believe this is also a root cause behind the staggering divorce statistics among churchgoing Christians and the growing carnality across the land.

How can we fight "the good fight" and stand strong against our enemy Satan when our spiritual vital signs are precariously low? How can a church make a positive impact on its community when it can't even get its own members to pray together? One of the keys to the church and the people God blesses is that they understand and follow the directions God himself gave for maintaining spiritual vitality and strength.

How can we be other than what we eat? How can God's grace work powerfully in us when we cut ourselves off from the very food he has prepared for our souls? Only one-third of all churchgoing, professing Christians read their Bibles even once a week! Is it any wonder why they are spiritually sluggish and easy prey for Satan's attacks? The practice of private prayer and collective praying together as a church has dropped to an all-time low in too many places. No wonder congregations are barely surviving and have no bold and powerful gospel witness to unbelievers. We can be spiritually "alive" yet be in an almost comatose state.

God has clearly promised that "he satisfies the *thirsty* and fills the *hungry* with good things" (Psalm 107:9), but how can we experience these blessings if we never sit down at his table and eat? Our natural bodies know the satisfaction and delight of eating a good meal, but what happens to our inner man that has no interest in steak and potatoes? No wonder so many Christians feel unsatisfied and unfulfilled. Our "spiritual man" can only be nourished when we partake of God's Word and receive the refreshing that comes from his Holy Spirit.

This lack of spiritual well-being also explains why there is so little praise and far too much complaining in our lives. How few can identify with the psalmist's words: "My soul will be satisfied as with the richest of foods; *with singing lips my mouth will praise you*" (Psalm 63:5). Just as people rave about a gourmet meal and pay tribute to the chef who prepared it, so should God's people be continually singing the praises of the One who feeds them daily with "the richest of foods." A church blessed by God is a joyful, loud, singing place, for how could it be anything else? When we "taste and see that the LORD is good" (Psalm 34:8), we will wholeheartedly join with the praiseful, "singing lips" of the psalmist no matter our personality type or denominational background. What a shame that many Christians get more excited and vocal about football games or an ocean cruise than about Jesus Christ, the Lord of heaven and earth!

GROWING IN SPIRITUAL MATURITY

There are other telltale signs when people are spiritually undernourished. Have you ever wondered why some believers live in a state of perpetual spiritual infancy and never grow up? What they take in spiritually is at the heart of the problem. First Peter 2:2 gives us God's nutritional guidelines for spiritual growth: "Like newborn babes, crave pure spiritual milk, *so that by it you may grow up* in your salvation."

Many pastors know the frustration of trying to help people who claim to have been Christians for years yet have all the maturity of a bunch of toddlers who get upset when someone takes away their crayons. Believers who don't continually drink the pure milk of the Word of God remain babyish and unstable because they are neglecting the spiritual food that will help them grow. How cruel it would be to deprive a newborn baby of milk and cause him or her to suffer horribly as a result. But think of all of God's "newborn babies" who are stunted in their spiritual growth because they *deprive themselves* of the pure milk their spirit craves.

This principle goes deeper still when we contemplate the multitudes who drink "spiritual milk" but never get off the bottle. How ludicrous it would be to see a thirty-five-year-old person sucking on a bottle and eating a jar of baby food. But that's exactly what can happen spiritually if we don't maintain a balanced spiritual diet. The apostle Paul warned the Corinthian church of this danger: "I gave you milk, not solid food, for you were not yet ready for it. Indeed, you are still not ready" (1 Corinthians 3:2). There was more for the Corinthians to learn than just the first principles of Christianity, but the believers there were too immature and worldly to digest "solid food" from God's Word.

To grow into spiritual maturity, we need to be conscious every day of the needs of our inner man and the scriptural reminder that "it is good for our hearts to be strengthened *by grace*" (Hebrews 13:9). God's grace comes in different forms and through various channels, but the truth remains the same. When we neglect such things as Bible reading, prayer, worship, and fellowship with other believers, problems of one kind or another will ensue as surely as night follows day. How can we ever be other than what we take in?

To grow into spiritual maturity, we need to be conscious every day of the needs of our inner man and the scriptural reminder that "it is good for our hearts to be strengthened by grace."

No one is more aware of this truth than Satan. The part of spiritual warfare that so few of us think about is the demonic strategy of cutting us off from our food supply. Satan knows that a "strong-in-the-Lord" believer is one thing and a weakened, emaciated one is quite another. Because of this, Satan uses a host of distractions, discouragements, and "junk-food" substitutes to keep us from receiving the daily nutrition our spirits vitally need. He will try to get us too busy, too tired, too discouraged—too anything—if only it will keep us from fellowship with the Lord and his Word.

Although we might be unaware of our most important calling from God, Satan knows all too well that we have been *"called . . . into fellowship with his Son Jesus Christ"* (1 Corinthians 1:9). Not everyone is a pastor, teacher, or missionary, but all of us have been called to derive our spiritual strength from a life of daily fellowship with Christ. Satan uses anything to keep us from communion with God so he can weaken us and soften us up for his next attack.

Is it any wonder, then, that the Lord urgently calls out to his people to carefully listen to this message? "Come," he invites us, *"come to the waters."* He pleads with each of us to let our heart reach out and take action so our soul can be satisfied. He invites us to come to the place of refreshing so we don't starve and shrivel up. He has provided all we need. The river is flowing. The waters are plentiful. The table is set. But we must take the time to receive what God freely offers, or it all counts for nothing. What good is the "richest of fare" if no one sits down to enjoy it? God's heart cries out, "Why spend money on what is not bread, and your labor on what does not satisfy?" Why live on the junk food of worldly entertainment and be preoccupied with "making it big" in some profession when all of it leaves you empty and unfulfilled?

Perhaps Satan is trying to block you from receiving the grace of God. If so, don't believe the lie that says you're not worthy, not ready, or not smart enough to come to his table. God is saying, "Come and get it!" It's all free and waiting for each of us because of his great love for us. Those who daily "eat" of God's Word and regularly "drink" of the Holy Spirit will experience the truth that King David wrote about centuries ago: "*Taste* and see that the LORD is good. . . . The poor will eat and be satisfied" (Psalms 34:8; 22:26).

It is amazing how deep the spiritual hunger and thirst can be in someone's soul. But how wonderful it is to find the true satisfaction through Christ that meets every longing within us. Earlier I mentioned Maria and the marvelous physical turnaround she recently experienced. But long before her life was transformed physically, she was changed more wonderfully—and it didn't involve a visit to a doctor's office.

NIGHTMARES AND DEEP SCARS

Maria's mom and dad were married for twelve years before she was born. The anticipation of their first child brought great joy, but during this time Maria's mom developed terrible headaches. By the time she was five months pregnant, the headaches had become so severe that her husband would find her banging her head against the wall and sometimes incoherent. Medical tests revealed a cancerous brain tumor, and at only twenty-nine years of age Maria's mom underwent major surgery.

She did not survive the surgery. The tiny, two-and-a-half-pound baby did.

This left Maria's dad in an impossible situation and so totally devastated emotionally that he could not even name his new daughter. Maria's birth certificate had no first name on it; a nurse actually named her.

Maria spent her first few months of life in the New York Foundling Hospital, where she suffered several physical complications. Her dad then brought her home and hired a nanny. But when

Maria was two and a half years old, he placed her in an expensive Roman Catholic boarding school. This was the best he could do. There she would at least be provided for physically, emotionally, and educationally and would receive strong religious training. Or so he thought.

Appearances were deceiving. Maria experienced great cruelty at the hands of the staff. A cat-o'-nine-tails and punching were part of the physical abuse, but that was just a small part of her nightmare. The emotional abuse was horrific. She was told that she was there because God knew "she didn't deserve a mother." Then there was the sexual abuse. Maria would wake up in the middle of the night completely naked, and a female staff member would be naked beside her. Nightmares and deep emotional scars were the inevitable results of such mistreatment of a frightened, frail, little girl.

The staff carefully covered up the physical beatings, but an unannounced visit by Maria's dad brought everything to light and ended her stay at the boarding school. He had been taking Maria home only on the weekends, but now the preteen moved in with him permanently.

It was a huge transition to go from the regimented life of the boarding school to the relative freedom of an apartment on the Lower West Side of Manhattan. Life on the streets was tough, but at least she was with her dad. Maria was so frightened of being "given away" again that at first she went to great lengths never to cause a problem for her father. During her second day at school she broke her thumb in a fight, but never told her dad even though the recovery was slow and extremely painful.

Maria secretly felt like a misfit because almost none of her peers lived in single-parent homes. She also was insecure about anyone caring enough to protect her. In an effort to fit in, eleven-year-old Maria started sniffing airplane glue and hanging out with the wrong crowd of kids. At age twelve she began drinking, and by thirteen she was smoking pot. Then her life really began to unravel.

Once Maria played hooky from school and went to a nearby movie theater. A policeman spotted her and pulled her into the theater manager's office, where she was lectured about the importance of getting an education. Unfortunately, the cop left too soon, and the theater manager sexually victimized her. It surely seemed as if Maria couldn't get a break in life.

"PARTY TIME"

By the time Maria was sixteen, her drug use had escalated to quaaludes, "uppers," "downers"— anything that would take her away from reality. At eighteen she was shooting heroin and getting high on "acid," mescaline, and anything else she could lay her hands on. Her life became a series of near disasters as she survived a gas explosion, was hit by a car, attempted suicide once, and overdosed three times. One fateful day she came home to find her dad dead in the apartment. Maria never even had a chance to apologize to him for all the aggravation and grief she had put him through.

Maria soon became a regular at disco clubs and after-hours nightspots in the city. (She was so intent on partying nonstop that she even found a club that was open on Sunday afternoons.) She met and started living with a guy named Michael Durso, who came from an upper-middle-class background. He seemed to be the answer to all her problems, and she fell deeply in love with him. But as time went on, the same, old, empty feelings within her surfaced again. She could find nothing to satisfy them.

FACING EMPTINESS

Michael and Maria went on a "honeymoon" to Mexico even though they weren't legally married. Maria smuggled two thousand dollars' worth of drugs with her to make their getaway at a Club Med all they hoped it should be. One evening Michael decided to go for a walk. Once again Maria was left alone to face her emptiness. Here she was, in a beautiful resort in Mexico, surrounded by loads of jewelry, clothes, and designer luggage. Yet she was absolutely miserable inside. For about the first time in her life, she began to talk to God. As she did, she became angry. In frustration she began to yell at Whoever might be listening, "What kind of God are you? Why am I alive and so empty and sad?"

Suddenly Maria heard a voice speaking to her heart! Gently it said, "Give me your life before it's too late." Although she didn't even know what those words meant, she decided to follow as best she could the new desires she was discovering.

Suddenly Maria heard a voice
speaking to her heart! Gently it said,
"Give me your life before it's too late."

As soon as Michael returned, Maria announced that she wanted him to go to church with her when they got back to New York. He was so puzzled that he told her to quickly smoke a joint so she could get her head back together. This wasn't the Maria he knew. Maria—going to church? Maria was the woman who wore those string bikinis, sometimes had a shaved head, and was always ready to party and get high. In Michael's mind, Maria and God did not seem to go together in any way, shape, or form.

Maria was so subdued during the last few days of their vacation that Michael wasn't sure their relationship had a real future even though they had just moved into a nice apartment in Brooklyn.

Upon returning to New York, Maria realized she needed to call someone to even find a church to visit. During her entire life she had never once heard anyone explain the gospel. If she and her friends accidentally switched on a Billy Graham television crusade, they dismissed the whole thing as another religious scam with money at the bottom of it. But now Maria felt compelled to get to a church, so she called a friend named Barbara.

After saying hello, Maria and Barbara simultaneously said to each other, "I need to talk to you."

Maria went first and bluntly told Barbara about her newfound sense of needing God.

"Praise the Lord!" Barbara exclaimed. This startled Maria because she had never heard that phrase before. Even more surprising, her good friend, of all people, was using it!

Barbara quickly explained that she and a couple dozen friends had all recently accepted Jesus Christ as their Savior. They also had gathered together and prayed specifically for Michael and Maria—the same night Maria had sensed God speaking to her heart. Barbara recommended a church in Brooklyn, and Maria eventually persuaded Michael to come with her.

Although Michael took it as a joke and half-mocked what was going on, Maria knew she needed what she felt in that church. At the end of the service, the pastor asked who was certain they would go to heaven if they died that evening. Maria knew she had no such confidence, so she walked forward to surrender her life to Christ. God was obviously up to something very wonderful because Michael was no longer mocking. Just as convicted about his need for Christ as Maria, he went forward with her!

JESUS' LIFE-CHANGING POWER

The young, spaced-out couple who went to a simple gospel meeting that Sunday night were totally transformed from their previous lifestyle. The things of God and eternity replaced the momentary pleasures of sin. Michael and Maria Durso now pastor Christ Tabernacle, one of the finest churches in New York City (and a "daughter church" of the Brooklyn Tabernacle), and God is blessing their ministry together. We had the privilege of sending them out to begin the work some fifteen years ago, and we still provide spiritual oversight.

Today Maria travels a considerable amount of time, speaking at women's conferences and churches as she shares the life-changing power of Jesus Christ. The fragile young woman who went down so many dead-end streets is now much more than a survivor. Through Christ she has become "more than a conqueror" (see Romans 8:37) and will never live with the gloomy mindset of a "victim." She has experienced firsthand what a wonderful table the Lord has set before her. She also knows that his goodness and mercy will follow her all the days of her life and that she will dwell in the house of the Lord forever (Psalm 23:6).

Lord, help us to value and enjoy the table you have prepared for us. Give us the discipline and desire to take in the Word of God daily. Let it dwell in our hearts and transform the way we think. Fill us over and over again with your Holy Spirit as we pray, worship, and wait before you. Make our churches strong and healthy in Christ. We ask all of this in Jesus' name. Amen.

THREE

Heaven's Guide to Proper Fashion

I grew up around what I call "clothesline religion." The leaders of the church my family attended placed tremendous emphasis on outward, legalistic standards laid down by the denominational headquarters. Even the smallest details of personal dress were regulated. My mother told me, for example, that decades ago when seamless stockings were the newest thing, they were loudly condemned as being "sensual." Women who wore anything other than seamed stockings were even in danger of facing church discipline. Oddly enough, years later when seamless stockings became the norm, the same men preached against the evils of seamed stockings that were then considered to be "alluring." If all that seems confusing, it was. Legalistic rules are hard to lay down and even harder to enforce.

The church in which I grew up wasn't the only place where dress codes were a big item. My grandmother (on my father's side) was part of a group that made my family's church seem like part of Hollywood. Her "bishop" (or pastor) forbade people to wear red clothes of any kind or open-toed shoes. Other prohibitions included chewing gum, men's hair that was long enough to "touch the ear," married couples wearing wedding rings, and men growing any facial hair. One time when I was twelve years old, my grandmother exploded at me while I was eating some raisins because they came from the same grapes that produced wine—and everyone knew what that could do to you! (Sometimes when I behave dysfunctionally, I ask my wife to be understanding because I obviously grew up around some very strange stuff.)

All the extremes aside, it is important for the Holy Spirit to teach us the meaning of what God does clearly say about outward apparel in such passages as 1 Timothy 2:9: "I also want women to dress modestly, with decency and propriety." It is obvious that, given the moral pollution in our society and the extreme sexuality common in much of the fashion industry, Christian men and women who want to please the Lord often will have to go against the tide. What the world calls "sensational" is often an abomination to our holy Father.

Through the years a number of visiting pastors and speakers have made interesting remarks about the way the congregation at the Brooklyn Tabernacle dresses. It surprised me the first time someone mentioned it, since I had never thought much about it, but similar comments have been repeated many times since. These ministers point out that although the church is located in the inner city and most of its members are not well-to-do, the believers who worship every Sunday in one of our four services look very attractive as a whole. In general the ladies come dressed smartly and modestly; the men are as well groomed as their circumstances permit. Many of these pastors have complained to me that in their own churches this is not the case. Inappropriate and even suggestive attire is commonplace, and people often make little effort to look clean and neat.

We all know that God is more interested in the hearts of his people than he is in their outward appearance, but it is probably wisest for us to look the best we can on the outside. Although a church service should never be a "fashion show," inappropriate dress can be both distracting and not helpful to the worship of God.

DRESSING APPROPRIATELY IN GOD'S SIGHT

I've become convinced that on a far deeper level many believers today are not dressing themselves appropriately in God's sight. This problem should be of special concern to the church that wants to experience all of God's blessings. I believe that even people who regularly attend Christian churches are dressing with little or no awareness of heaven's guide to proper fashion, and this negatively affects the growth of God's kingdom on earth.

What am I talking about? Listen to this: "Therefore, as God's chosen people, holy and dearly loved, clothe yourselves with compassion, kindness, humility, gentleness, and patience. . . . And over all these virtues put on love, which binds them all together in perfect unity" (Colossians 3:12, 14).

In this important chapter the apostle Paul exhorted the Christians in the church in Colossae to be what they are in Christ. Since God had raised them into a new life in Christ, they needed to keep setting their "minds on things above, not on earthly things" (Colossians 3:2). After all, their new and permanent source of joy and peace would be found only where "Christ is" (v. 1).

As members of God's family, they also needed to "put to death" old, sinful inclinations and rid themselves of the evil habits they used to practice (v. 5). Paul pointed out that this was only logical, since at the time of their conversion they had "taken off" their "old self with its practices" and had "put on the new self, which is being renewed . . . in the image of its Creator" (vv. 9–10).

Please notice the important imagery of "take off" and "put on." This is in keeping with the idea of being dressed spiritually according to God's plan for our lives. How unseemly it is for us as Christians to be "dressed" like something we're not while we decline to "put on" the beautiful wardrobe the Lord has provided for us.

*How unseemly it is for us as Christians to be
"dressed" like something we're not while we
decline to "put on" the beautiful wardrobe
the Lord has provided for us.*

COMPASSION

The first item on heaven's dress list is to "clothe
yourselves with compassion." God's idea of
spiritual fashion and attractiveness begins with
tenderhearted pity and mercy toward other
people. One Bible translation renders the word
compassion as "a deep feeling of interest," which
stands in stark contrast to the cold, insensitive,
and self-preoccupied attitudes of society in
general. When self-interest is not involved, most
people could care less about the plight of others.
How different such an attitude is from that of our
Savior, who, "when he saw the crowds, . . . had
compassion on them, because they were harassed
and helpless, like sheep without a shepherd"

(Matthew 9:36). Jesus looked beyond people's surface appearance and even the sinful habits that dominated their lives. He saw into their hearts and felt compassion for their feeble, confused state.

Many of us feel that discerning the faults of others is a sign of our spirituality. Nothing could be further from the truth. The real mark of Christlikeness is to be stirred in our hearts by what others are going through. It is to be moved in our hearts by the inner battles with sin and the feelings of inferiority and guilt that people fight day after day.

It is easy to give up on people when we see them continuing down the wrong road, but what if Christ had responded that way toward us? Remember, we all came from the same cesspool of sin. Rather than looking away from our horrible condition, Jesus showed great compassion and even gave his life for us. How ungrateful it is of us to wear the clothes of insensitivity and self-righteousness when the only reason we are in the family of God is that "the Lord is full of compassion and mercy" (James 5:11).

KINDNESS

The next thing we are to put on is "kindness," which brings a warmth and softness to our spiritual appearance. The spirit of kindness gives the church God blesses a very inviting atmosphere. Who doesn't appreciate kind people who do and say kind things? In contrast, is there anything more uncomfortable than being around a sour, bitter person whose words and actions reek of unkindness? Kindness denotes a sweetness of social intercourse that brings blessing and encouragement wherever it goes, and it was one of the magnetic qualities of Jesus while he was on earth. Jesus was kind and considerate to everyone he met, and we who bear his name also should be known by our kind disposition as we represent him to others.

D. L. Moody, the great evangelist of the nineteenth century, said that the hardest thing for God to do was to make a man kind. I think he was right. Many of us memorize Scripture and understand Christian doctrine, but we ruin our witness because we are unkind in our conversations and dealings with other folks. We have an "edge," for whatever reason, that makes us and our faith unattractive to the very people who need to be drawn to the Lord.

How easily we forget the wise advice the elders gave King Rehoboam at a crucial moment in Israel's history: "If you will be kind to these people and please them and give them a favorable answer, they will always be your servants" (2 Chronicles 10:7). But the new king was too arrogant and full of himself to listen to such counsel, so he reacted poorly and spoke with extreme unkindness to the people. The result? A civil war divided the twelve tribes of Israel for centuries and led to intermittent fighting that cost countless lives. Oh, the terrible price we sometimes pay for our unkindness! No wonder Scripture warns us that "a kind man benefits himself, but a cruel man brings trouble on himself" (Proverbs 11:17).

How different would our lives and churches be if we followed the apostle Paul's advice to "make sure that nobody pays back wrong for wrong, but always try to be kind to each other and to everyone else" (1 Thessalonians 5:15)? There is no excuse for us to be unkind or bitter because another person has behaved toward us in an unkind fashion. Is that the way God responded when we spurned his voice and rejected his offer of salvation? No. In fact, it was God's kindness that drew us toward him. We must never forget that God still uses kindness to draw people to himself.

"Love is kind" (1 Corinthians 13:4). Wherever God's Spirit is working and blessing, there will always be the sweet fragrance of kindness. But this attitude is not easily maintained. Everyone knows, for example, that it is difficult to be kind to ungrateful or wicked people. We are naturally repelled by those who never express appreciation and have nasty personalities. But with God all things are possible! Our Lord will help us show the world how deep and true his love is by enabling us to be kind to everyone we meet. We can rise, through Christ, above the petty pattern of being unkind to unkind people. Then we can rest assured that our "reward will be great, and [we] will be sons of the Most High, because he is kind to the ungrateful and the wicked" (Luke 6:35).

HUMILITY

The well-dressed Christian still has more to put on in order to follow the Lord's example. "Clothe yourselves with ... humility" is the next instruction from God's Word. This humble mindset gives us a low opinion of ourselves, and only the Holy Spirit can provide us with such a rare garment. It is so easy to be proud because of what we feel are our superior talents, possessions, or achievements. Pride is so subtle that even when folks are dirt poor and have very great limitations, they can still be very full of themselves.

When we live with a proud attitude, we are susceptible constantly to the tension and disappointment that accompany it. Every little remark or negative comparison is like a painful pinprick to our inflated egos. When we put on pride, it takes a lot of energy to be always defending and reestablishing our superior position in the minds of everyone we meet.

Real humility, not the feigned kind, begins when we think and feel about ourselves according to truth. Just the simple truth about God, ourselves, and life is all we need. All we have to do is ponder the truth about our past failures and sins, our incredible limitations, and the fragile nature of life itself. If we spend a little time alone with the Lord confessing these things, we will be well on our way toward having a new spirit of humility in our daily lives. If, on the other hand, we live in falsehood and fantasy about ourselves, then we put back on those out-of-date, ugly clothes we once wore during our former lives before we came to know Christ. After all, since Christ, the Son of the living God, was "gentle and humble in heart" (Matthew 11:29), isn't it morally insane for people like us to be proud? What do we have that the Lord didn't give us? Every talent we have, every success in life . . . it has all come directly from his gracious hand.

The first secret to receiving guidance from God is a humble spirit.

The church God blesses must always maintain a humble position before God and man. Any feeling of superiority ("we're the best church around") or arrogance in the pulpit will quickly grieve the gentle Holy Spirit. The congregation and leaders who understand the need for humility and pursue it will never fail to be led down the right path because "he [God] guides the humble in what is right and teaches them his way" (Psalm 25:9). The first secret to receiving guidance from God is a humble spirit.

The congregation acquainted with the spirit of humility will continue to draw strength from God's unlimited supply. They will humble themselves not only before God but before one another. The apostle Peter wrote, "All of you, clothe yourselves with humility toward one another, because, 'God opposes the proud but gives grace to the humble'" (1 Peter 5:5). How wonderful it is to be among believers who, rather than fighting for prominence as the world does, desire only to serve one another in lowliness and love.

Humility is probably the rarest article of spiritual clothing found among the people of God. Pride, however, is plentiful and grows at an amazing rate. Pride is like a junkyard dog that can feed on anything—including the blessings of God! If we are not careful, even answers to prayer can move us away from the position of lowly dependence on the Lord, which is where we need to stay. It seems that often when a crisis has passed, our once lowly hearts begin to reassert themselves. How easily we begin to think we're somebody special when we're really not. So let us put off the heavy, prickly garments of pride and put on Christ, "who, being in very nature God, . . . made himself nothing. . . . And being found in appearance as a man, he humbled himself" (Philippians 2:6–8).

GENTLENESS

Gentleness, the next spiritual garment we need to put on, is not featured in Vogue or GQ magazine, but heaven still puts great value on it. Gentleness has to do with a spirit of submission that prevails during the trials of life, especially in relationship to God's dealings with us. J. B. Phillips translated gentleness as "the grace to accept life." Gentleness is the opposite of the harshness that comes from a frustrated heart full of turmoil. Things don't always work out as we hoped, and sometimes the bottom falls out of our best plans. Life certainly has its disappointments—and that's where gentleness comes in. God's grace can help us to accept these disappointments—large and small—so that we can move on in an attitude of gentleness, exhibiting trust and meekness. When we don't put on gentleness, we dishonor Christ daily by venting our irritation as if God isn't aware of our situation and has permitted our world to spin out of control.

Jesus is the example of gentleness we are to follow. Think of how he preached while the religious leaders on the edge of the crowd plotted his demise, the fickle masses so slowly understood the truth he taught, and his inner circle of twelve disciples argued about who among them was the greatest! Unjust attitudes and accusations dogged his every step, yet he remained gentle and serene through it all.

How different it often is with us. Just let one of us buy a new car that turns out to have some defects, and we are ready to go up in smoke. And think of all the people who go through each day with silent anger because things haven't worked out for them and they think life has been "unfair." But God can deliver us from these old, carnal ways and help us to gently accept things as we remember that "the steps of a good man are ordered by the Lord" (Psalm 37:23 NKJV).

PATIENCE

Patience is like a perfectly matched mate to gentleness and involves being long-suffering with others. Not only do the events of life challenge us, but people can get on our nerves, too. When family members, friends, or even acquaintances let us down, we need to run quickly to God's wardrobe and put on some divine patience. I say "divine" patience because in ourselves we all too easily become resentful toward those who accidentally or purposely injure us. But the church God blesses lives with a consciousness of how patient the Lord has been with them—over and over again.

Even among fellow Christians there will sometimes be problems and hurts. That is exactly why Paul wrote, "Bear with each other and forgive whatever grievances you may have against one another" (Colossians 3:13). Our immaturity often causes us to react by saying, "Hey, how could they do that? I thought they were Christians!" How childish it is to think that in this life we won't have to deal with complaints, differences, and quarrels from time to time!

Whenever someone acts or talks inappropriately, God has given us another opportunity to obey this command: "Be patient, bearing with one another in love" (Ephesians 4:2). Why would this admonition about "bearing with one another" be in the Bible unless God knew there would always be things that are hard to bear? (In fact, just take one ride on a New York City subway and you will know why God put this verse in the Bible: "Be patient with everyone" [1 Thessalonians 5:14]).

Being patient with everyone might seem difficult for us, but from a heavenly perspective how can we not be patient? When we silently seethe against someone who hurt us and harbor resentment for decades, the angels in heaven must be tempted to take off their halos and scratch their heads. How can they not be puzzled? We were once in rebellion against God, yet he waited patiently for us to turn away from our sin. Some of us cursed, lied, and violated every holy commandment of our loving God. He could have obliterated us, but instead he showed incredible patience. He was long-suffering with us. He waited for us to come to him. Even after coming to faith in Christ, we have stumbled and fallen more times and in more ways than anyone except God and us can know. But still, in love, he patiently picks us up as a loving father would a frail child. Surely the angels stand perplexed that sinful people to whom the holy God has shown such patience could be so resentful of others who have "failed" them and then justify their silent bitterness on top of it!

Each of us has experienced God's love in a way that should soften our hearts and make us sweet and long-suffering even toward the unkindest people.

Oh, let us run quickly to the throne of grace so we can put off the horrible rags of resentment against anyone and put on the patience of Christ! Each of us has experienced God's love in a way that should soften our hearts and make us sweet and long-suffering even toward the unkindest people. From the pulpit to the newest believer in Christ, the Brooklyn Tabernacle is filled with examples of God's grace. And no one better illustrates divine patience than Edgar Ramirez.

SPIRITUAL DARKNESS, SPIRITUAL LIGHT

Edgar grew up in an inner-city home that was half heaven, half hell. He had a godly, praying mother and a violent, hard-drinking dad who physically abused his wife in front of Edgar's young eyes. Edgar's father was the incarnation of the verse, "Wine is a mocker and beer a brawler" (Proverbs 20:1). As Edgar grew older, fear turned slowly into hate in his heart, and he angrily vowed revenge. But his precious mom never lost her faith in Christ, and she tried to instill the same faith in her son.

Edgar's daily Bible readings and prayer with his mom stood in stark contrast to the witchcraft and idolatry Edgar's dad practiced in the same home. Sacrifices of fruit and money were made to his dad's physical idols, which became, in time, like part of the furniture. But light conquered darkness when Edgar gave his heart to the Lord at the age of twelve.

Because of the bitter wrangling at home, young Edgar was relieved when his father joined the merchant marine. This meant that his father was away at sea three to six months at a time. His father's absence brought peace into the home and more opportunities for Edgar's mother to raise her son in the ways of the Lord.

Edgar became involved in a local church and at age fourteen had a remarkable experience with the Holy Spirit. The teenager gained a new burden for souls, and he and a friend named Franky began to witness boldly to gang members around the Sunset Park area of Brooklyn. But Satan had a plan to derail Edgar's faith in the Lord. Oddly, it was two men in the church whom the enemy used. A youth leader, of all people, introduced Edgar to marijuana. Then a minister tried to sexually molest him. Both of those events, along with a false accusation made against him, caused Edgar to grow very hard inside.

Sadly, Edgar turned his back on the Lord, and a spiritual darkness seemed to descend upon him as he reached his later teenage years. Drugs, wild parties, sex, anger, and brawling took him far away from the path upon which his praying mother had once set him. On top of everything else, or maybe at the bottom of it, Edgar became intensely cynical about every minister with whom he came in contact.

One night Edgar and his cronies were plotting a ten-thousand-dollar robbery of a bakery chain. They closely followed the van that picked up the money from the various stores and awaited their chance near the Hunts Point Market. But that very night, Edgar's mom felt impressed to pray fervently for her wayward son. At the last second, something went wrong and the criminal plans had to be scuttled. But the chaos inside Edgar still raged.

Edgar had never forgotten the pain his father inflicted on the family, and while he was home from overseas his dad began once again to horribly abuse his mom. This pushed Edgar over the edge. He soon got a seven-inch knife, which he planned to stick into his father's heart. Needing a little help to carry out this mayhem, Edgar spent a whole night getting high. Then he came back to the apartment and walked slowly toward the room where his father slept. Abruptly Edgar felt an urge to turn on the television. A Christian evangelist appeared on the screen, and the first words Edgar heard were, "Why are you going to commit such a horrible act? Don't you know that your life is worth saving? Jesus loves you!" The Holy Spirit used these words to pierce Edgar's heart. He gave up on committing his horrible act of vengeance, but continued to rebel and turn away from God.

As a result of his promiscuous lifestyle, Edgar was diagnosed with herpes. This, along with the patient pleading of the Holy Spirit, brought Edgar to the end of himself. After several hours of heavy drinking, he ended up one Thanksgiving eve underneath the beautiful Verrazano-Narrows Bridge on the southwestern tip of Brooklyn. There, all alone, Edgar wept and repented his way back to Christ. Years of horrible behavior were washed away by the loving God who had never given up on this angry, confused young man.

And that is what "long-suffering" is all about. In fact, that is what Jesus Christ is all about, as the apostle Paul revealed. Considering himself "the worst of sinners," Paul explained that his conversion was the opportunity for Jesus to once again show his "unlimited patience as an example for those who would believe on him and receive eternal life" (1 Timothy 1:16).

Edgar is now married to a beautiful woman named Maria, who also deeply loves the Lord. They have three children. Edgar's fear of infecting his family with the virus has never materialized. The children are all healthy and serving the same God who answered, in the end, the prayers of a humble Puerto Rican mother on her knees at the throne of grace. The child for whom she interceded has grown up to have the hand of the Lord upon him and is anointed by the Holy Spirit to speak, pray, and lead others by word and example.

The dramatic turnaround in Edgar's life is a vivid reminder for all of us to "be kind and compassionate to one another, forgiving each other, just as in Christ God forgave you" (Ephesians 4:32).

Father God, we thank you for your mercy and patience toward us. We ask in the name of Jesus that you will teach us daily to put off all that belongs to our former, sinful way of living. Help us also to put on those things that belong to Christ—his compassion, kindness, humility, gentleness, and patience. Fill us over and over again with your love so that people will see your likeness in our lives. Amen.

FOUR

The Hinge That Opens Heaven's Door

Sometimes the most intricate or powerful machinery can become totally inoperative because of a missing or broken part or a faulty connection. Although its potential remains tremendous, the broken machinery is good for nothing.

Another way to think of this same principle is to consider how even the most enormous doors swing open and closed on relatively small hinges. Although the hinges are mostly out of sight and unimpressive in comparison to the door, the door's proper operation is vitally dependent upon those hinges. An unhinged door cannot function as a door. In the spiritual realm, there is also something that, when absent, shuts down the gracious operation of the Holy Spirit and wastes the great potential of both the individual believer and local congregations. Even though people may be in relationship with the Lord, the Bible gives us some disastrous scenarios that can occur when things became spiritually unhinged.

THE ISRAELITES' DISTRESS

Consider, for example, the case of the Israelites. They were mightily delivered from the bondage of slavery in Egypt. God raised up Moses to be their leader, and nothing Pharaoh and his armies did could stand before the power of Jehovah. After the Israelites wandered for forty years in the desert of Sinai, God raised up Joshua to lead the people. By God's power they crossed the Jordan River into the Promised Land, a land that was rightly named because God's promise to Abraham hundreds of years earlier was being fulfilled (Genesis 17). By divine decree, God ceded the land to Abraham's descendants. God instructed the Israelites to boldly drive out all the Canaanite nations because he himself would fight for Israel!

Well, if both God's promise and power were on the side of the Israelites, how is it that we read these words not long after Joshua's death? "He [God] sold them [the Israelites] into the hands of the Philistines and the Ammonites, who that year *shattered* and *crushed* them. For eighteen years they *oppressed* all the Israelites on the east side of the Jordan in Gilead.... Israel was in *great distress*" (Judges 10:7–9). Why did this tragic and unthinkable reversal in Israel's fortunes occur? Weren't the Israelites the chosen people of God? Weren't they under covenant with the Almighty? Didn't the pagan Philistines and Ammonites worship dumb, powerless idols? There's something seriously wrong with this picture!

As we probe deeper for an explanation, we discover that God himself was behind the entire matter. "*He* sold them into the hands of the Philistines and the Ammonites"! How could God have turned against his own people? As always, we look in Scripture to find the cause: "Again the Israelites did evil in the eyes of the LORD.... And *because the Israelites forsook the LORD* and no longer served him, he became angry with them" (Judges 10:6–7).

Persistent, unconfessed sin was the reason behind Israel's stinging defeats at the hands of the Philistines and Ammonites. Persistent, unconfessed sin was the cause of Israel's submission to an idolatrous people who easily could have been defeated otherwise. Persistent, unconfessed sin was at the bottom of the whole mess, just as it is throughout all of sacred Scripture. The Israelites did evil, and God's promises and power were short-circuited by the people's ungodly behavior.

Even as we gain insight into the cause of Israel's pathetic plight, we find in this passage a statement of even greater importance: "Then the Israelites cried out to the LORD, '*We have sinned* against you, forsaking our God and serving the Baals [idols]'" (Judges 10:10). Again they cried out, "'*We have sinned*. Do with us whatever you think best, but please rescue us now.' Then they got rid of the foreign gods among them and served the LORD. And *he* [God] *could bear Israel's misery no longer*" (vv. 15–16). We have just read about the great spiritual hinge that opens the door of heaven.

As soon as the Israelites honestly *confessed* their sins and repented, God went from selling them into the hands of their enemies to quickly raising up a warrior leader, Jephthah, who subsequently reversed the fortunes of God's people. "Then the Spirit of the LORD came upon Jephthah. . . . Then Jephthah went over to fight the Ammonites, and the LORD gave them into his hands" (Judges 11:29, 32). From defeat to victory, from slavery to dominion—it all hinged on the simple act of sincere confession of sin.

From defeat to victory, from slavery to dominion—it all hinged on the simple act of sincere confession of sin.

Israel didn't add more soldiers or more sophisticated weapons to its inventory; the Israelites simply confessed their sin, and God moved over to their side. They didn't need any new promises. They didn't need any new prophecies. They simply needed to get right with God by confessing from the depth of their hearts, "We have sinned." Until they took that step, God's hand *had* to oppose his own people. Otherwise he would have been encouraging them to continue down an evil path that leads to every misery known to man.

GOD HATES SIN

Now, I know that dealing with sin isn't a politically correct concept to examine in these shallow, user-friendly days, but let's do it anyway. *God hates sin.* That's the best place to start because it is the essential fact about all sin. God's holy nature detests every kind of sin. He is grieved and provoked by sin, as we see over and over again in the Bible. Sin, and nothing else, is what separates man from God. This is why Christ shed his blood, endured the cross and its shame, and went through the agony of being God's sacrificial Lamb. He did it all to deal with the ugly fact of sin in your life and mine.

In the end, God will annihilate all sin. He cannot relent from this because it is the essence of his holy nature. Through Jesus he provided for the washing away of sin's guilt. Through the presence of the Holy Spirit within us, he provided an antidote to sin's power over us. But always remember that in the end God will destroy the

very fact of sin in the universe so that righ-
teousness and peace can reign eternally.

It is obvious, then, that our first order of
business as Christians every day is to deal with
sin. Daily, hourly, and moment by moment, we
must by the grace of God bring all our sin to the
Lord in sincere and contrite confession. Confession of sin is the most important key to being a
people and church that lives continually under the
blessing of heaven. Once unconfessed sin begins
to fester in our hearts and lives, there is absolutely
no telling what sad chapters will be written even
though we claim to be the people of God.

Our need to confess sin exposes the whole
fallacy of "positive confession" (a teaching that
you can have from God whatever you say) or the
recitation of certain prayers as if they are a magic
mantra for success. If there is unconfessed sin
and a clogged-up spiritual life underneath everything, we can recite Scripture all day and claim
every promise in the Bible, but God is bound by
his own Word not to answer us. Psalm 66:18
states, "If I regard iniquity in my heart, the Lord
will not hear" (NKJV). This truth brings out in
bold relief not only the awful effect of sin but

also the incredible power of confessing our sin openly to a loving Savior.

Confessing our sin leads to the greatest spiritual joy and peace we can experience as human beings. The psalmist David, who was an expert in these matters, described it this way:

> Blessed is he
>   whose transgressions are forgiven,
> whose sins are covered.
>   Blessed is the man
> whose sin the Lord does not
>   count against him
> and in whose spirit is no deceit (Psalm 32:1–2).

Notice that David didn't say, "How blessed and happy is the man or woman who has never sinned," because that would leave no chance of blessedness for anyone who has ever lived.

Confessing our sin leads to the greatest spiritual joy and peace we can experience as human beings.

David went on to tell us about his own experience with sin: "When I kept *silent*, my bones wasted away through my groaning all day long. For day and night your hand was heavy upon me; my strength was sapped as in the heat of summer" (vv. 3–4). Here this anointed servant of the Lord was going through a very hard time because of God's displeasure and relentless pressure against his disobedience. We aren't sure of the exact circumstances to which David refers, but we are certain that God's "hand was heavy upon" him as long as he kept silent and unrepentant about his sin. Instead of the inner peace and joy he so often sang about in the Psalms, he felt a horrible, dry, and parched condition in his soul.

As we read on, we see a sudden reversal in David's pathetic situation: "Then I acknowledged my sin to you and did not cover up my iniquity. I said, '*I will confess my transgressions to the Lord*'— and you forgave the guilt of my sin" (Psalm 32:5). It's as if David said, "Why do I continue to live under the Lord's displeasure? I may not be able to *undo* my sin, but *I can confess* it to the God of my salvation." At the very instant he made a true confession, David found abundant mercy and pardon waiting for him.

David's experience and that of the Israelites in Judges are two examples of the incredible power and privilege we have as the children of God. We can—daily, hourly, and moment by moment—confess our sins knowing that God will forgive us and chase away the dark clouds that hover over our spirits.

The great danger is for us to cover up sin, lessen the seriousness of it, or justify our behavior because of "special" circumstances. We must also avoid dealing selectively with our sin by confessing certain acts of disobedience while we cling to other attitudes and habits that are especially dear to us. Satan uses each of these natural tendencies to keep us from the mercy of God. Open and complete confession of sin brings it to the only place it should go—to God, who can forgive and take our sin away.

REAL CONFESSION

Real confession means to *say the same thing about sin that God says*. Real confession involves humbling ourselves and *agreeing with him* about the very nature of our sinfulness. To live under the blessing of heaven is to always be running toward God with our guilt and not away from him (as if we could ever hide from him anyway). As we renounce our sin and turn from it, we give it up with full confidence that God will act in accordance with his Word. He *will* forgive freely. He *will* cleanse us from every stain of sin. He *will* help us because of his great love.

But let's be careful to deal thoroughly with our sin, because God can never alter his holy opposition to it. What we call "little sins" might be easily excused, but we are deceiving only ourselves. Why lose God's best for our lives and dishonor him by permitting little foxes to spoil the vine? Let us ask his help in confessing every kind of disobedience, no matter how inconsequential it might seem.

Remember God's eternal promise in 1 John 1:9: "*If we confess our sins,* he is faithful and just and will forgive us our sins and purify us from all unrighteousness." The problem is not with the Lord's ability or desire to forgive and purify us; it is in the word *if. We* must confess agreement with God's view about our sin and turn from it as something we do not ever want near us.

Without this careful dealing with sin, our lives and our churches will become hollow and lifeless. We may continue an outward observance of Christian ritual, but we will be strangers to the power and blessing that have been promised by God. When confession of sin is seen in its true light and is practiced by a humble, contrite people, there will always be a fresh release of the Lord's grace among us.

In recent decades many believers have rediscovered certain biblical truths. The second coming of Jesus Christ has been preached and written about more during the last one hundred years than during all the preceding centuries put together. The importance of worship among Christians has been newly emphasized also. Praise choruses and recordings abound across the world. These truths are very important, but they cannot even be compared with what God can and will do when confession of sin is brought back to its vital and rightful place among us.

Honest confession of sin undergirds and makes genuine all the other things we do as Christians. How deep can our praise and worship be if the people lifting their hands and singing have made a treaty with sin? And what good are all the Christian books and sermon tapes if they never get to the heart of the matter—the reality of our sin in the eyes of a holy God?

God has faced the problem of unconfessed sin with his people many times. Much of the book of Hosea is about the sad plight of Israel when the people would not give up their sin no matter what God said or did for them. The Lord loved his people dearly and expressed this over and over again as he called them back to himself. He even threatened severe remedial action, saying that he would become "like a lion to Ephraim [Israel], like a great lion to Judah. I will tear them to pieces and go away. . . . I will go back to my place" (Hosea 5:14–15). What a terrible consequence for the people of Israel: The blessing and special presence of Jehovah himself would go away as part of a divine strategy.

And what was the strategy? What was the aim of these strong, corrective steps taken against his very own? "Then I will go back to my place *until they admit their guilt*. And they will seek my face; in their misery they will earnestly seek me"

(v. 15). The whole point was to get the Israelites to admit and confess their sin. The emptiness God wanted to heighten among them by his going "away" was only to cause them to face up to their sins. Once they admitted their guilt, a brand-new channel of fellowship and blessing from God would be opened.

Please remember, this entire process of discipline was carried out against the chosen people of God. The Lord was not a "lion" tearing to pieces the nations of Moab or Egypt. He was a "lion" to his own wayward children who needed to confess their sin. And so it remains to this day.

As Peter wrote in the New Testament, "For it is time for judgment to begin with the family of God" (1 Peter 4:17). Of course it must begin with the family of God! How will unbelievers be convicted of their sin and turn to Christ if the people who are preaching the gospel deal fast and easy with their own sin? Or, more to the point, how can the Holy Spirit effectively carry out his work through a church that permits unholy things in the lives of the congregation?

The church God blesses must maintain a holy guard against the cancerous nature of sin. Sermons and exhortations cannot omit this important truth just because it makes some people feel uncomfortable. We must remember that wonderful things happen when sin is brought out into the open and confessed.

Consider what happened in Ephesus about two thousand years ago when "many of those who believed now came and openly confessed their evil deeds. A number who had practiced sorcery brought their scrolls together and burned them publicly" (Acts 19:18–19). Was this bonfire an unnecessary, melodramatic touch, or did it serve an important purpose? The Bible makes a clear connection between such a radical dealing with sin and the spiritual results that followed. "*In this way* the word of the Lord spread widely and grew in power" (v. 20). When confession and carefulness about sin prevail in the church, so will God's will prevail in the spreading of the gospel of Jesus Christ.

The worst possible scenario is for our churches to be supposedly "growing" but with "members" who have no deep longing to be delivered from the power of sin. That situation will fulfill the New Testament prophecy of "terrible times in the last days" when people will have "a form of godliness" but live every day "denying its power" (2 Timothy 3:1, 5).

The worst possible scenario is for our churches to be supposedly "growing" but with "members" who have no deep longing to be delivered from the power of sin.

We all know how easy that can begin to happen in our own lives and churches. We can attend services regularly and even read the Bible without getting to the root problem on which God is putting his finger. An incident from my life serves as a reminder of how important it is to deal with sin no matter how insignificant it may seem to be.

STEAK AND A BAKED POTATO

Carol and I had been married only a few months and were both working in New York City. The furthest thought from our minds was that we might someday pastor a church. We were a typical, newlywed couple living in a tiny apartment in Brooklyn.

There are many adjustments you have to make when you are first married, and I wasn't mature enough to make some of them well. One day after we came home together on the subway from work, Carol was good enough to cook one of my favorite meals—steak with a baked potato and vegetables. The only trouble was, I like steak on the rare side and what she put in front of me tasted like a piece of well-done shoe leather. This disturbed me because Carol *knew* how I like steak cooked. In my immaturity I made a less-than-complimentary remark to her. She had experienced a long day at the office and was in no mood for my lack of appreciation of her culinary skills, so she gave me a less than pleasant reply. This provoked me to say some unkind words, which resulted in a classic, newly married couple's spat. The meal was ruined. (My precious steak went down the drain!) And the atmosphere was no longer love and kisses.

I was determined to have the last word, and determined that it would be a righteous one at that! I declared that I was going to the midweek church service that night and added that not even a burnt-to-a-crisp piece of steak would keep me from my devotion to Christ! Not surprisingly, I went alone. And I justified my behavior all the way to the church door. I listened as best I could to the sermon, but then the pastor called the few believers present to come to the altar for a season of prayer. That's when my dilemma came to a head.

I knelt down and was silent for a while. To say that the skies above me were like brass would be an extreme understatement. Instead of having faith to lay my needs before God, all I could sense was my hardness of heart and guilt for my sins. Almost immediately I sensed God speaking deep within me: "Get up, go home, tell her you were wrong, and say you're sorry!" This was not exactly what I had in my mind when I made my way to church. Didn't God understand the extreme cruelty of a burned-up piece of meat? Was this really the Holy Spirit speaking to me, or a false spirit from the pit of hell? How could anyone who loved me ask me to do such an impossible thing as saying "I'm wrong" and "I'm sorry" all in the same night?

I disregarded as best I could what I felt God was saying to me. I tried hard to pray, but I was between a rock and a hard place. The One whose help I needed was the very One who had a controversy with me, and he would not relent! All I could hear over and again as I knelt at that altar was, "Get up, go home, tell her you were wrong, and say you're sorry!" Finally, I gave up pretending to pray and went home as directed.

While driving home, I still argued about the unfairness of the whole situation. I was willing to do a lot of things for the Lord, but I thought he was really being unreasonable. I would have put all my money into the offering basket. I would have visited the sick and shut-in folks. But to confess my sin openly to my wife, of all people, and then apologize on top of it—well, that was a cross far too heavy for a mere mortal like me to bear. My proud and sensitive soul could not accept why *I* had to be one who came crawling!

I quieted down a bit while walking to the apartment after parking my car, and my heart became very tender as I ascended the one flight of stairs to our door. As soon as I opened it and walked down the hallway, tears began to flow.

Before I could call out to Carol, she was already heading toward me. As I reached out my arm to hold her, I sobbed out as best I could, "I'm so sorry, I was so wrong to talk that way. Please forgive me." Carol then said with brokenness that she was also sorry for how she responded. (She didn't need to say that because I knew I was the real culprit.)

If someone had seen us embracing like that in a half-lit hallway, they never would have understood the depth of what was transpiring. As I spoke aloud my confession of failure and sin to my wife and to God, the blessings of God poured down upon me like a river of fresh water on a dry desert. Peace and joy welled up together as my tears became a language that I knew God understood, because it was to him and not Carol alone that I was speaking. And I can tell you from firsthand experience how true the psalmist was when he wrote,

> Then I acknowledged my sin to you
>   and did not cover up my iniquity.
> I said, "I will confess
>   my transgressions to the Lord"—

and you forgave
   the guilt of my sin.
Therefore let everyone who is godly pray to
    you
   while you may be found;
surely when the mighty waters rise,
   they will not reach him (Psalm 32:5–6).

FRESH BLESSINGS

This powerful truth applies to all believers and every Christian congregation. When we honestly confess our sins, we clear the way for fresh blessings to come upon us from the Lord. It is possible that right now you are sitting in the shadows rather than in the sunlight of God's favor. The only thing in the world that can keep you there is unconfessed sin. Why live one minute longer in that condition when a loving, merciful God is calling you into fellowship with him? Don't put it off another day. Use David's prayer for mercy as a help as you go to the throne of grace.

Have mercy on me, O God,
   according to your unfailing love;

according to your great compassion
   blot out my transgressions.
Wash away all my iniquity
   and cleanse me from my sin.
For I know my transgressions,
   and my sin is always before me. . . .
Hide your face from my sins
   and blot out all my iniquity. . . .
Restore to me the joy of your salvation
   and grant me a willing spirit, to sustain
      me.
Then I will teach transgressors your ways,
   and sinners will turn back to you (Psalm
      51:1–3, 9, 12–13).

FIVE

HEART PROBLEMS

While I was writing this book, my wife and I were visited by her Uncle Mel and his wife, Phyllis, from Portland, Oregon. Mel Arn grew up on a dairy farm in Wisconsin and became a Christian at a young age. His zeal for the Lord and spiritual things, especially prayer, never flagged and was still evident during his stay at our home. He was eighty-one years old, physically full of vigor, and did daily push-ups to help keep himself fit!

Yesterday, before I began writing this chapter, we received a phone call that Mel had gone to be with the Lord. He had returned home from his trip "back east" and was excited and grateful that he had visited with so many old friends and family members. Then he simply went to bed and during the night was ushered into the presence of the Lord. An old soldier full of prayer and devotion to Christ, he entered into his eternal reward. While he slept that last night, his heart simply stopped beating. No matter how fit you are for your age or how many vitamin supplements you take, when your heart stops working, your life ends.

Although physical heart problems claim many victims each year across our country, there are heart problems of another kind that I want us to consider. The heart is also of critical importance in a *spiritual* sense. The church, and especially the pulpit that God blesses, has to have a unique kind of *heart*. I believe the heart factor is the most overlooked aspect of all our sincere searching for keys to living successfully for Jesus Christ.

Whenever we think about the ministry of a Christian pastor, teacher, or evangelist, our minds turn to the example set by the apostle Paul. Whenever we analyze the building of an effective Christian church, our thoughts again turn to Paul, the "expert builder" (1 Corinthians 3:10), who by the grace of God laid the only true foundation and built wisely upon it. No one in the Bible had such insight into the blessing of God upon both the ministry and the church as the apostle Paul. This is illustrated by the fact that his life after conversion dominates the book of Acts, and most of the epistles (letters) of the New Testament were written by him. No one had deeper insight into the gospel and the mystery of divine grace than this man who went from being a Jewish zealot who persecuted believers to being the greatest ambassador for Jesus the world has ever seen. So if we want to experience more of God's power working through us, we must study carefully the life and ministry of this great Christian.

Because of his great impact, more books have been written about the apostle Paul than any person in Scripture other than Jesus Christ. In these volumes two very important aspects of Paul's phenomenal ministry have often been analyzed: his message and his method.

PAUL'S MESSAGE

First, the *message* Paul preached is essential to our understanding of him. His main focus was always the *gospel,* or good news, about Jesus Christ. In fact, Paul saw his calling as an apostle to be centered in the "priestly duty of proclaiming the gospel of God" (Romans 15:16). Paul, unlike Moses, was not a preacher of merely the *law* of God. The apostle certainly used the holy commandments in his message, but it was only to prepare the minds and hearts of his audience for the message of Christ. Paul also proclaimed the *promise* of salvation and a new life through Jesus. He was "not ashamed of the gospel, because *it* [the gospel!] is the power of God for the salvation of everyone who believes" (Romans 1:16).

Paul didn't ask his listeners to make promises to do better or to make commitments to turn over a new leaf. That will never bring the liberating power of the Holy Spirit, because those vows are characteristic of the law of Moses, not the gospel of Jesus Christ. The apostle understood, as few others ever have, the truth that "the law was given through Moses; grace and truth came through Jesus Christ" (John 1:17). The church

God blesses is a *Jesus church*, a church that recognizes that he is the only answer to the need of the human heart. A Jesus church is a place that proclaims the *good news* concerning salvation, not merely the law of God that can convict of sin but does nothing to lift a soul out of its despair. It is a congregation that is excited about the Lord Jesus and provides living proof of the dynamic power that is experienced when people repent of sin and put their faith in Christ. That was the message of the apostle Paul.

PAUL'S METHOD

Second, the *method* of Paul is revealed through his movements and ministry as traced through the book of Acts and his letters. The odd thing about this subject is that Paul knew little about *methodology* as we use the term. The apostle was a Spirit-led man from start to finish. He depended on the guidance of the Holy Spirit for what he was doing and for what to do next, and we can discover no church-growth formula from his life. His ministry was characterized more by divine anointing than by clever methodology.

*What he did then for Paul he will
do for us as we yield our hearts to
him and learn to listen.*

Even Paul's plans to evangelize in certain areas were subject to the Holy Spirit's intervention. "Paul and his companions traveled throughout the region of Phrygia and Galatia, having been kept by the Holy Spirit from preaching the word in the province of Asia" (Acts 16:6). This is one of the beautiful secrets of the church and ministry God blesses. The people know that God's desire to lead his people by the Spirit has not changed, so they seek to remain sensitive to his voice. How else can God's people accomplish God's will except by being led by God's Spirit? Who wants to mechanically follow dead church traditions or man-made formulas when we can have God take us by his hand and guide us?

Being led by the Spirit was not an unusual experience for Paul, as we see in the next verse:

"When they came to the border of Mysia, they tried to enter Bithynia, but the Spirit of Jesus would not allow them to" (v. 7). Paul was not planning a vacation in Bithynia. He was planning to preach the gospel in a province that needed to hear it. Even so, the Spirit of Jesus had other plans for the apostle, and he obeyed in childlike fashion. Oh, how we need to follow the example of Paul's tender submission to the promptings of the Holy Spirit! Others may call such devotion fanaticism or emotionalism, but the people God blesses believe their Bibles. They know that the Holy Spirit has not changed one iota in two thousand years. What he did then for Paul he will do for us as we yield our hearts to him and learn to listen.

PAUL'S MOTIVATION

As important as the apostle's message and methods were to his spiritual success, there is one more piece to the puzzle. I am convinced that Paul's motivation (or heart) is the most overlooked and least-taught-about aspect of his ministry to people. Are there not countless churches today that proclaim the gospel of Christ from their pulpits, yet make little, if any, impact on their communities? Their doctrine and message are biblical, but the results are meager compared with the apostolic model. Are there not many congregations that confess belief in the present-day ministry of the Holy Spirit? Yet even when this belief is part of the doctrinal statement, we do not see the kind of gospel proclamation that cuts to the heart of the hearers and brings multitudes into God's kingdom. This brings us to the heart of the matter, which happens to be Paul's heart.

Read carefully as Paul reviews his ministerial style and motives to the church in Thessalonica:

> We speak as men approved by God to be entrusted with the gospel. We are not trying to please men but God, who tests *our hearts*. You know we never used flattery, nor did we put on a mask to cover up greed—God is our witness. We were not looking for praise from men, not from you or anyone else (1 Thessalonians 2:4–6).

Paul took his calling as a preacher of the gospel quite seriously. It was a sacred task, fulfilled with a deep desire for God's approval. That longing for God's approval is always true for the ministry God blesses. There is no place in God's work for impressing people with clever oratory or using flattery to get on their good side.

The apostle wasn't looking for money and had no secret motive to fleece the flock. He wasn't interested in selling books, becoming famous, or receiving accolades from the people he spoke to or anyone else. Then what was his motivation as he toiled among them?

> As apostles of Christ we could have been a burden to you, but we were *gentle among you, like a mother caring for her little children. We loved you so much* that we were delighted to share with you not only the gospel of God but our lives as well, because you had become so dear to us (1 Thessalonians 2:6–8).

What a radical picture of a minister these words present to our modern minds! The apostle reminded his readers of the passionate heart of love he had as he labored among them. He was "gentle . . . like a mother caring for her little children." The picture presented here in the original Greek is that of a mother tenderly bringing a baby to her breast to be fed and nourished. The apostle boldly declared that he wasn't ready just to give the gospel message but to give his very life as well. That is why he described himself as having the heart of a mother who so cherishes her children that no sacrifice is too much if only it will bring blessing to her offspring.

This was the motivation behind Paul's preaching and gospel work in the church in Thessalonica. No wonder his sermons had a bite to them and reached the hearts of the people. His message didn't come from an educated intellect alone, but from the fervent love that burned within his soul. No wonder he didn't care about their money or applause. It was all about them and their welfare, just as it always is when a mother is caring for her children.

When God blesses a pulpit and church, the heart of the pastor and congregation must be in proper working condition. Selfishness and "comfort zone" religion must be replaced by the same sacrificial love God gave to Paul. How can people powerfully preach the message of Christ without having the tender spirit of Christ inspiring them?

In fact, if I am writing this book to become well known or to profit financially, then I prostitute the high calling of a minister. (And woe to me when I have to stand before God in the end.)

Isn't the right kind of heart the crucial need among our churches today? Too many people in the ministry are driven by their desire for fame and fortune, but how many have you met who are ready to give their very lives for the people to whom they minister? Isn't this lack of fervency the reason why so much of our work, sermons, and activities produces so few dramatic conversions from darkness to light? The message might be correct biblically, but the spirit of the message hasn't captivated our souls, so it has little impact on the souls of others.

Paul went on to reveal more about the inner workings of his heart: "But, brothers, when we were torn away from you for a short time (in person, not in thought), out of our intense longing we made every effort to see you. . . . [That sounds more like a gushing love letter than a minister writing to a congregation!] For what is our hope, our joy, or the crown in which we will glory in the presence of our Lord Jesus when he comes? Is it not you? Indeed, you are our glory and joy" (1 Thessalonians 2:17, 19).

This language is, again, foreign to our ears but very refreshing at the same time. The apostle cherished the people in Thessalonica so dearly that to be away from them put a great strain on his emotions. It was with "intense longing" that he tried to see them again face-to-face.

Why did he so treasure that new congregation and think of them constantly? It was simply because they were his great hope, joy, and crown when Jesus Christ would return again to earth. These believers were the trophies of grace that he would present to God on that inevitable day of judgment and reward. Even though Paul experienced a vision of the risen Christ and wrote most of the New Testament, his "glory and joy" were the ordinary people who had become Christians through his ministry. He was far more excited about them than he was about any material possession or personal achievement.

TROPHIES OF GOD'S GRACE

Recently my book *Fresh Wind, Fresh Fire* was named Book of the Year by the Evangelical Christian Publishers Association. When Christ returns, would I be foolish enough to wave this honor before him as something significant in the light of eternity? After all, he is the one who wrote the Bible! Will my wife, Carol, hold up one of the Grammy awards she has received? No, our great crown and joy in that day can only be people whom we have led into the kingdom and ministered encouragement to as they followed Christ. All of our church buildings, gorgeous sanctuaries, and plush carpeting will be burned up in an instant. Nothing but the flesh-and-blood trophies of God's grace will shine on through eternity.

The church God blesses keeps its focus on this one thing—the people for whom Christ died and their progress in the faith. This is why Paul made tremendous sacrifices and took great personal risks. It was all because he was head over heels in love with God's people. Mechanical preaching and corporate-like thinking never entered his mind when building the church of Christ. Men, women, boys, and girls who had put their faith in Jesus would be his great joy, hope, and crown in the day of Jesus Christ.

But there is still more to this Holy Spirit—given passion that beat within the apostle's breast. Paul sent Timothy to Thessalonica to get news about the spiritual state of the believers he so loved. He charged Timothy to strengthen and encourage them in their faith because of the inevitable trials they would face as Christians. "But Timothy has just now come to us from you," Paul wrote, "and has brought good news about your faith and love" (1 Thessalonians 3:6). Young Timothy reported to the apostle that the believers in Thessalonica were standing strong in Christ. Paul's reaction to this excellent news elicited one of the most stunning passages in the entire New Testament: "Therefore, brothers, in all our distress and persecution we were encouraged about you because of your faith. For now we really live, since you are standing firm in the Lord" (vv. 7–8).

This is the heart God blesses! Paul can endure all kinds of personal distress and persecution with joy if only he is certain that his beloved flock stands firm in the Lord. What does it matter what he goes through as long as they are healthy and strong in their faith?

That was the motive of ministry that made Paul so unique. Yes, his gospel message and Spirit-led methods were critical factors, but his heart was like that of the Lord himself. Paul's love for God was proven real because it expressed itself in a life passionately lived for others. Possibly the greatest spiritual deception we can fall into is to think we really love the Lord while having little concern for his people. Knowledge of scriptural truth and interest in the workings of the Holy Spirit mean absolutely nothing if, in the end, we can't say, "Now I really live since you stand firm in the Lord."

Possibly the greatest spiritual deception we can fall into is to think we really love the Lord while having little concern for his people.

A lack of motivation to sacrifice for others is what holds back many ministries and churches from being greatly used of the Lord. Biblical truth is memorized by the mind, emotions are occasionally stirred by the things of God, but it all doesn't go deep enough to transform our motive for living. Only the Holy Spirit's power can save us from the terrible plight of a self-centered, comfort-zone lifestyle while we sing hymns about the Christ who gave his life on Calvary. Unless damage—serious damage—is done to our self-life, religion like that becomes nothing more than a charade. The acid test of spiritual growth is love, and love always means living for others.

This type of Christlike ministry is so rare that even Paul could not produce many like-minded workers. The problem is, you can't teach or impart this kind of passionate concern. It must come directly from the Holy Spirit working deep within a person's soul. As the apostle wrote about the band of workers and preachers who traveled with him, note his revealing comments in Philippians 2:19–21: "I hope in the Lord Jesus to send Timothy to you soon, that I also may be cheered when I receive news about you. I have no one else like him, who takes a genuine interest in your welfare. For everyone looks out for his own interests, not those of Jesus Christ."

The Philippian church was also very dear to Paul's heart, but only Timothy had the apostle's confidence when it came to deciding who should be sent to encourage and strengthen them. When Paul wrote, "For everyone looks out for his own interests," he was not referring to pagan unbelievers but to his own ministerial team! Preachers and workers of a certain type he could easily recruit, but only Timothy had a kindred spirit that would take "a genuine interest in your welfare."

I can still vividly recall when, as a novice pastor, I was stunned when I first encountered the egotism and materialistic attitude of some ministers. An opportunity to preach in front of an audience, along with a guaranteed love offering or honorarium, was their only concern. Taking time to labor in prayer with people or to offer a personal word of encouragement was of no interest to them. They were performers rather than ministers in the apostolic mold. And those kind are still very much with us today. Let us pray that God will raise up pastors, congregations, Sunday schools, and choirs that are motivated by the same kind of love the apostle Paul had. The Holy Spirit can still fill us with this divine love so that no sacrifice will seem too much as we spread the gospel to those for whom Jesus Christ died. J. W. Tucker had a heart like that.

A SPECIAL HEART

In 1928, at the close of a gospel service in Russellville, Arkansas, a thirteen-year-old boy named J. W. (Jay) Tucker surrendered his life to

Christ. He was very sincere in his devotion to the Lord and grew up to be a godly example to others. At the age of twenty, Jay entered a Bible school in Oklahoma and, while there, felt a distinct call from God to be a missionary to Africa.

The words rang clear and true in his heart: "Are you willing to go to Africa as a missionary?" And the slender young man with a tender heart answered, "I am willing, Lord."

A friend of his planned to go to West Africa upon graduation, but Jay felt the Lord calling him to Congo. Since the door to Congo seemed closed, Jay decided to accompany his friend to West Africa. At the last moment, however, a sudden change in circumstances made possible his fervent desire—Jay Tucker was going to Congo to share the good news of Christ.

Jay was part of a group of seven Congo-bound missionaries on their way to Belgium for language study when the outbreak of World War II disrupted their plans. They all felt their only option was to go directly to Congo. Application problems and other obstacles seemed insurmountable, but God helped them, and on October 28, 1939, Jay and the six others finally set sail for Africa on the

SS Exeter. At that time there was only one way to reach their destination. From Alexandria, Egypt, they traveled by boat and train southward through Sudan toward the Congo border. One of the other missionaries in the group, a young lady named Angeline Pierce, was later to become Jay's wife and co-laborer. The long arduous journey provided much time for their relationship to blossom.

Upon their arrival in Congo, Jay and the other missionaries attended their first conference of resident missionaries and Congolese believers. Some came from hundreds of miles away, and their spirited singing and enthusiastic welcome touched Jay deeply. This is my land, he thought, my chosen people, and he immediately went to work acclimating himself to his new home.

During those early months Jay was a builder, student, teacher, and preacher—all at the same time. As the years passed, his sense of calling only deepened, as did his love for the people. Because of legal requirements in Congo, Jay and Angeline had to travel to Uganda, 325 miles away, as their long-anticipated wedding date neared. She had made a lovely white, satin gown. He wore his Bible school graduation suit. On April 10, 1941, the couple were united in marriage. Although they did not have many material possessions, they had one another and their shared sense of God's hand upon them for ministry.

After six years in Congo, Jay and his wife returned to the United States for an eighteen-month furlough. They then returned to Congo and once again threw themselves into serving the people in the name of Christ. Two sons and a daughter were added to the family as their years of dedicated service for Christ rolled by. In 1958 the Tuckers were asked to move their family to a new ministry center in the city of Paulis. It was difficult to find space for a home in Paulis, and even harder to find a place to begin church services, but the Lord provided. Starting in a backyard area, the new church grew quickly to more than a hundred members. But hanging over the city and the entire country was a deep sense of unrest as talk of independence spread like wildfire.

After months of deliberations with Belgian officials, the nationalist movement led by Patrice Lumumba gained strength, and independence was soon won. Almost immediately, there were uprisings against the resident Belgians, and many gathered their families and fled the country. The

Tuckers felt that as nonpolitical missionaries they would be safe and decided to stay in Paulis even though the tension heightened each day. Soon all the local missionary women and children were airlifted from Congo to Uganda. Three weeks later, Jay came and brought his family back to the Congolese congregation he loved so much. Things quieted down for a while, and the Tuckers were overjoyed when authorities sold him a lot in the city where a new church could be erected.

Political disturbances never totally ceased, however, and trouble always seemed imminent. Eventually European and American consuls advised their citizens to leave because hatred toward foreigners increasingly flared into acts of violence. The Tuckers again sent their children to a school in Kenya but remained in Paulis, ministering the Word of God until 1963, when a much-needed furlough to the States was scheduled. Six hundred Congolese Christians came to say farewell to the couple who had shown them such love and concern. "Bwana! Madamo! Please come back," they called.

Back in America, the Tuckers followed closely the news from Congo. Things seemed peaceful again, but the Tuckers felt apprehensive about returning to Congo with three children. "I must go back," Jay told his wife one day. "God is calling me back. We must trust him. We have trusted him for twenty-five years. It must not be different now." So, in August 1964, the Tucker family returned to Paulis.

They received a warm reception from missionary friends and Congolese believers, but the city was already in a state of unrest. Rebel forces were threatening government troops in nearby areas, yet everyone felt sure that they could never take control of Paulis. Just two weeks before the children were to be taken to boarding school, rebel forces did the unthinkable. They entered the city and brought death and carnage everywhere. Dead bodies littered the streets as the Tuckers anxiously waited for events to unfold. Jay was taken in for questioning several times, but he was always released safely.

Soon things turned even more grim. The Tuckers' car was confiscated, and they were put under house arrest with soldiers posted outside their door. Jay was arrested on November 4, along with dozens of others, and was held in the Catholic Mission. The rebels grew violent and began marauding through the streets. On November 24 a rebel band came to the mission and dragged Jay Tucker and the other prisoners out into the streets. Using mainly gun butts and beer bottles, the rebels hacked and clubbed the dedicated missionary and twelve others to death. It was reported that Jay's screams could be heard for blocks as the angry mob took some forty-five minutes to kill him. The next day his body was thrown into the back of a truck and hauled fifty miles into the jungle, where his bloodied remains were tossed into the croco-dile-infested Bomokandi River. Two days later, on Thanksgiving Day, Belgian paratroopers rescued Angeline Tucker and her three children and trans-ported them out of Paulis.

GOD'S PERFECT PLAN

It seems tragic at first glance that twenty-five years of compassionate ministry for Christ should end in such a horrid manner. How could the life of Jay Tucker be taken by a Congolese mob in the very city to which God had sent him? This true account may seem somewhat strange in a book about the ministry and church God blesses. When laid next to the doctrinal perversions of the "name it and claim it" prosperity teachers, the life and times of Jay Tucker certainly seem meager and wasted. But now, as they say, let's hear the rest of the story.

The Bomokandi River flowed through the Nganga region of Congo, where the Mangbetu tribe lived. The Mangbetus had remained totally resistant to any penetration of the gospel. Even the famous missionary C. T. Studd was never able to win one Mangbetu convert. Another mission group followed up on his efforts, but not one Mangbetu turned to the Lord.

A unique Mangbetu traditional saying:
"If the blood of any man flows in our
river, the Bomokandi River,
you must listen to his message."

As the Congo rebellion subsided, the king of the Mangbetus persuaded the central government in Kinshasa to send a chief of police to bring stability to the region. The government sent a man of strong stature who was known simply as "the Brigadier." What no one knew was that the Brigadier had been won to Christ by Jay Tucker a few months earlier.

The spiritual environment the Brigadier encountered was one of total darkness, and the relatively new Christian found no response to his first attempt at sharing the gospel of Christ. Then one day the Brigadier heard of a unique Mangbetu traditional saying: "If the blood of any man flows in our river, the Bomokandi River, you must listen to his message." This saying had been part of tribal culture from time immemorial. Suddenly a thought came to the Brigadier. He summoned the king and village elders to meet him at a designated place for a special meeting. They respectfully gathered in full assembly to hear what he had to say:

> I want to tell you something. Sometime ago a man was killed, and his body was thrown into your river, the Bomokandi River. The crocodiles in this river ate him up. His blood flowed in your river. Now, before he died, he left me this message.

This message concerns God's Son, the Lord Jesus Christ, who came to this world to save people who were sinners. He died for the sins of the world; he died for my sins. I received this message, and it changed my life.

Now, if this man named Jay were here today, he would tell you this same message. He's not here, but his message is the same. And because this is the message of the man whose blood flowed in your river, you must listen to my message.*

As the Brigadier preached the simple message for which Jay Tucker gave his life, the Holy Spirit brought deep conviction. The light of the gospel began to finally shine through to the Mangbetus, and many were converted. Today in the Mangbetu region in northeastern Zaire (formerly the Belgian Congo), there are hundreds of believers and dozens of churches. They can all be traced back to the passionate missionary whose blood flowed in the Bomokandi River. His love for people led to his death, but in dying he brought the message of eternal life in a way he never could have imagined. And somewhere in heaven, it is very possible that

Jay Tucker is experiencing the same joy that the apostle had when he wrote these words: "How can we thank God enough for you in return for all the joy we have in the presence of our God because of you?" (1 Thessalonians 3:9).

> God, please forgive us for selfish living that gives little thought to the needs of those around us. Melt our hearts, and break us in the deepest part of our being. Flood us with your love so we can see and feel about others as you do. Save us from ourselves, and thrust us into the fields that are ripe for harvest. We ask this in the name of Jesus, who gave himself for us. Amen.

---

*The story of Jay Tucker is adapted with permission from the archival files of the Assemblies of God World Missions Department.

SIX

"BREAKOUT" POWER

The blessing of God always depends on the simple essentials of spiritual life. You don't need a seminary education or an especially gifted mind to learn the secret of his favor. In fact, a humble Christian in the most impoverished or limited circumstances can experience more divine blessing than a brilliant theologian surrounded by a vast library of religious books. It's the simple devotion of the heart, not complicated concepts, that opens up the windows of heaven's blessing upon our souls.

This is nowhere better illustrated than in the life of one of God's favorites in the Old Testament.

David went from being a simple shepherd boy to being the king of Israel because *God was with him*. Although God is omnipresent—existing everywhere in the universe at the same time—he is not *with* everybody in precisely the same way. So although no one can escape his presence as Almighty God, he definitely is *with* certain individuals and churches in the sense of supplying greater grace and blessings. This was the case with David, who faced tremendous odds and powerful enemies yet stood triumphant in the end because God's hand was with him. David's life is a vivid illustration of just how marvelous it is to live under God's special care.

We find one of the interesting secrets to David's unique relationship with the Lord in an obscure story in 1 Chronicles 14. David had survived more than ten years of being hunted by a jealous King Saul, who had recently died. God had watched over and protected David and promoted him at last to the throne of Israel—just as he promised when David was only a teenager. The new king had the support of all of the nation's twelve tribes. There was excitement in Jerusalem because "the LORD had established him as king

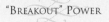
over Israel and . . . his kingdom had been highly exalted for the sake of his people Israel" (v. 2).

OUR RELENTLESS FOE

It is during this high tide of popularity and momentum for David that we read, "When the Philistines heard that David had been anointed king over all Israel, they went up in full force to search for him, but David heard about it and went out to meet them" (v. 8). What a great reminder this is for the church and people God blesses. No matter how wonderfully the Lord has worked on our behalf, spiritual enemies are still arrayed against us, and their spiritual attacks must be encountered until Jesus comes again!

These are the plain facts of spiritual warfare, and we would be wise to always keep them in mind. In fact, one of Satan's most strategic moments occurs when a great victory is won and we are on a kind of "spiritual high." The Philistines, for example, could not have cared less about the euphoria surrounding David becoming king or the fact that God's promise had come to pass. They came up in full force to search him out with only destruction on their minds.

That's the way Satan always is, and always will be, until he meets his final doom in the fires of hell. He is a relentless foe who knows that high, spiritual moments often relax our guard and cause us to be less vigilant against his approaches. There is a whole class of temptations in his arsenal that he reserves just for the times when we receive favor from the Lord. The Bible contains several tragic stories of people who fell into awful peril during the most blessed moments of their lives.

Let us ask God for more grace so that we can follow this scriptural warning: "Be *self-controlled* and *alert*. Your enemy the devil prowls around like a roaring lion looking for someone to devour" (1 Peter 5:8). Let us remember that experiencing God's blessing doesn't make us less of a target for the devil. In fact, it draws his special attention. But God is able to give us the victory over every satanic assault.

WE MUST SEEK GOD'S DIRECTION

There is much more to this episode than just the summary statement that the Philistines gathered

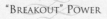

against David and he "went out to meet them." We want to focus on the "how" behind this sentence, as revealed in 1 Chronicles 14:9–10: "Now the Philistines had come and raided the Valley of Rephaim; so David *inquired of God:* 'Shall I go and attack the Philistines? Will you hand them over to me?' The LORD answered him, 'Go, I will hand them over to you.'"

This is an unusual series of events, when you think about it. David was at the height of popularity, and his veteran army was poised to defend the nation. Patriotic emotions and political excitement filled the air as God's anointed servant finally took his rightful place on the throne. On top of that, the Philistines were the enemy, and their army was routed years earlier by Israel when a teenage David slew their champion, Goliath. So the new king should just rush out with his army to do battle because these idolatrous pagans have no chance whatsoever against Jehovah and his hosts, right?

That is not what David did at all. The king humbled himself before God and requested divine direction as to whether he should fight *this* battle. Then he asked whether God would go *with* him in power so that the enemy would be defeated. David did not want to be in the wrong battle at the wrong time, so he inquired of the Lord who knows all things. Although he was God's anointed king and a veteran warrior, although the Lord had helped him countless times before, David would not move without God's approval and promise of blessing. No wonder David had such a special place in the heart of Jehovah!

There is no "automatic pilot" by which we can run our lives. We constantly need the Lord's direction as we face all the decisions of life.

Those of us who want to see God fighting *our* battles must pause and contemplate all of this very carefully. There is no "automatic pilot" by which we can run our lives. We constantly need the Lord's direction as we face all the decisions

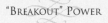

of life. We can't live off past successes either, because there is no guarantee that we will have God's approval and blessing on our next venture. Neither can we run around reciting "God is with me, God is with me," because the Lord was never *with* any king more than David, yet he still had to seek God for fresh instructions. If Jesus said, "The Son can do nothing by himself; he can do only what he *sees* his Father doing" (John 5:19), and testified that "whatever I say is just what the Father has told me to say" (John 12:50), then what do you think about our need to wait before God for instructions about life?

Another important truth in this narrative is that "the LORD answered him." What else would a loving, heavenly Father do but happily respond when his child comes before him in prayer with a humble and teachable spirit? Will he turn us, his children, away to fend for ourselves when he knows we want his direction and blessing? Is that even imaginable? Never! Somehow, in some way, the Lord will guide our steps in the way we should go. He will honor our desire to seek his will and blessing.

"So David and his men went up to Baal Perazim, and there he defeated them. He said, 'As waters break out, *God has broken out* against my enemies *by my hand*'" (1 Chronicles 14:11). David's careful prayer for God's direction resulted in a stunning victory over the Philistine forces. Although the king and his army waged war, it was David's own testimony that *"God has broken out* against my enemies." When we consult the Lord concerning *his will* for our lives and when we desire *his presence* above all else, the result will be *"breakout" power*. We will experience the awesome combination of *"God* has broken out" along with "by *my* hand." What an experience it is to have God working on behalf of his people while they fight on bravely in his name!

OUR GOD HAS "BREAKOUT" POWER

This is the kind of "breakout" power for which so many pastors across our country long. They are tired of leading mechanical services attended by lukewarm believers. They want to lead churches that God blesses so that communities can be impacted with the gospel and the person of Christ will be exalted. It is far better to live just a few years in that wonderful atmosphere

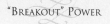

than to live through decades of wandering around in a spiritually barren wilderness.

God is ready to radically change things because no obstacle is too difficult for him. After all, the people called the place where David defeated the Philistines "Baal Perazim," which means "the Lord who breaks out"! Our God is a "breakout" specialist who delivers us from opposing forces and sets us at liberty to better serve him.

Possibly you face a dilemma of some kind today. Maybe it is related to your marriage or a son or daughter who is not serving God. Or possibly you need the Lord to heal you in the realm of your emotions. Whatever the case, remember that we have a God who can "break out" and supernaturally help us. And it all begins when we slow down and humble ourselves in prayer. We must bring our individual circumstances before God, as David did, with a yielded will that desires to know what *he* wants us to do. "Breakouts" begin not with noise and clamor but with a surrendered heart that asks, "Shall *I* go and attack the Philistines? Will *you* hand them over to me?"

CONTINUING OPPOSITION

But the conflict wasn't over. The enemies arrayed against David were very persistent. *"Once more the Philistines raided the valley; so David inquired of God again"* (1 Chronicles 14:13). The Philistines were not going to give up the fight just because they had been routed at Baal Perazim. Even as we must continually face opposition in the realm of spiritual warfare, David learned that the Philistines were once again on his doorstep.

You might automatically think that after having been so blessed by God and having recently crushed these same enemies, David would quickly race out to the battlefield and give them one more thumping. But the king's next action and its results are full of instruction for us. David inquired *again* of the Lord before he made a single move, even though the natural thing would have been to follow his instincts. But David wouldn't budge unless he *again* had God's consent.

God faithfully answered David, but added new and specific instructions as to how to fight *this* battle:

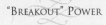

"Do not go straight up, but circle around them and attack them in front of the balsam trees. *As soon as you hear* the sound of marching in the tops of the balsam trees, *move out to battle,* because that will mean God has gone out in front of you to strike the Philistine army." So David did as God commanded him, and they struck down the Philistine army, all the way from Gibeon to Gezer (1 Chronicles 14:14–16).

What a faithful God David served! The Lord gave a *specific strategy* to his servant concerning deployment of troops against the enemy. For some unknown reason, David was not to make the typical, frontal assault that had gained the last victory, but was to circle around and amass his forces near the balsam trees. God also indicated the *timing* of Israel's attack—"as soon as you hear the sound of marching in the tops of the balsam trees." What humility and trust this story shows on the part of the king, and what a vivid illustration this is of God's great love. David didn't have to wonder, worry, or figure out things for himself. God proved again that he was the true "commander of the army of the LORD," as revealed to Joshua hundreds of years earlier (Joshua 5:14). Everything David needed to know concerning the battle was given to him—right down to the exact timing of the army's assault. Once again, God's presence went with David so that the victory was assured.

What is especially critical is the specific "word of the Lord" that answers the need of the moment and is what the Lord would say if he stood in the pulpit that day.

STAYING IN TOUCH

The living lessons for us are quite obvious. We must stay in close communion with our Lord if we are to enjoy his full blessing. Reflex responses based on past success are not adequate, because we need to *continually* seek God for fresh guid-

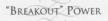

ance. We also need to be sensitive to the Lord's timing concerning our actions. Often we pursue God's *will* about something but don't have the faith to seek his *timing* for it as well. This story about King David was written in Scripture for our learning and encouragement. As we wait before the Lord, we will learn to "hear the sound" of the Holy Spirit's voice in our hearts and move out into God's perfect plan for us.

Too many of us pastors have no concept of this as we minister to people. For example, we feel that if our sermons come from the Bible, our message is adequate. We are blind to the fact that God alone knows what the enemy is secretly up to in the lives of the congregation. The Lord wants to direct us to the exact scriptural messages needed to thwart Satan's devices and lead the people to safety and rest. Circumstances will also change as time goes on, because the church is a growing, spiritual organism and the devil regularly alters his strategies. The saints of God must definitely be fed God's Word, but what is especially critical is the specific "word of the Lord" that answers the need of the moment and is what the Lord would say if he stood in the pulpit that day.

If God directed David to fight against the Philistines thousands of years ago, will he not also guide us in the way we should go? How can Christians ever think of changing jobs, moving to another state, or starting a business without inquiring of the Lord? God has detailed plans for every one of his children, and he would love to share those plans with us. How can churches hire employees or worship leaders choose music without giving a thought as to God's will and timing? Has Almighty God stopped caring about his children? Are we wiser and more spiritual than King David?

BREAKING HARDENED HEARTS

The Lord has dealt with me many times about the importance of knowing his will, and not all the lessons I have learned came when I anticipated them. An experience I had in Surinam, South America, twenty-five years ago still stands out vividly in my mind.

I ministered the Word of God at a pastor's conference in Argentina and then made my way north through Brazil so I could reach Paramaribo,

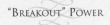

the capital of Surinam. (This former Dutch colony is quite small.) One of the largest churches in the city had invited me to preach, and I looked forward to seeing my Surinamese friend who pastored the congregation.

Even though it was February, temperatures were soaring as I was driven to the church for the morning service. A few ceiling fans turned slowly but did little to combat the stifling heat and humidity. After some preliminaries I was introduced to speak, and within ten minutes my shirt and suit were hanging on me soaked with perspiration. But the heat was the least of my problems that Sunday morning.

My sermon was bouncing back to me as if I were preaching to a concrete wall! The people were not inattentive, but a spiritual hardness permeated the atmosphere. I struggled mightily to get my message across. There was something in the air much more oppressive than the temperature and humidity. *What was wrong?* I didn't know, but it made me try harder, which only created more perspiration. (My light-blue suit was rapidly turning into a beautiful shade of navy blue.)

Since then I have preached in countless settings, nationally and internationally, but I can't remember a more difficult speaking situation. Something was *very* wrong, I felt, but what should I do to see a breakthrough? I started desperately praying in my heart even as I continued my sermon. (This is an excellent idea when you are thoroughly bewildered.) *God,* I prayed silently, *what am I up against here, and what can I do to bring a blessing to your people?*

My message soon ended, and I asked the people to bow their heads in prayer. As we quietly waited before the Lord, my own heart was still asking God for direction. I opened my eyes to look out over the audience, and suddenly my attention was drawn to a blonde, middle-aged woman sitting in the last row. I can't define what I felt, other than that I sensed the Lord focusing on her. Knowing I should follow this vague leading from the Holy Spirit, I called her out publicly and asked if she would come forward for prayer.

This turn of events seemed to slightly unnerve the congregation. (To be honest, I didn't know where it was going either.) The woman complied with my request, but as soon as she

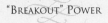

reached the alter area she broke down and began to weep. Soon many others walked forward to join her, and a prayer meeting broke out. Everyone's heart was melted. The atmosphere was transformed into something quite beautiful and heavenly.

As the organ quietly played a hymn, the Spirit of God "broke out" and created a 180-degree turn in the service. I prayed and wept along with the other people as a spirit of brokenness and contriteness settled upon us all. Toward the end of our prayer time, I noticed the woman going to the pastor and his wife. She hugged them for a long time, and many tears were shed.

I went to my pastor-friend's home afterward for dinner, and our hearts were rejoicing because of what God had done during the service. During the meal the pastor asked me why I called that particular woman forward out of the hundreds who were present. I explained as best I could, but he quickly filled in what was missing in my understanding:

"Brother Jim, our church has been suffering for months from a terrible outbreak of gossip and

slander. Our services have been hard and lifeless.
[I could bear witness to that!] Much of the nasty
talk has been directed against my wife and me. We
didn't know what to do because it has been so
painful. The one thing we did find out for sure was
that the woman you called forward was the ring-
leader and major source of this destructive talk.
When you called her out, it was as if God, through
a total stranger, had singled her out in a supernatural way. Some others involved with her sensed
that, and they were also convicted. She hugged us
at the end and begged for forgiveness. She confessed her sin and wants God to bring blessing to
both herself and our church. Praise the Lord!"

---

*A young, inexperienced preacher faced
difficulty he didn't know how to handle, but
God turned the whole situation around.*

Praise the Lord, indeed! A young, inexperienced preacher faced difficulty he didn't know

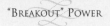

how to handle, but God turned the whole situation around. When I inquired of the Lord, he gave an answer that broke the stronghold of Satan and brought deliverance, too.

No wonder David rejoiced in the same faithfulness of God:

> I sought the LORD, and he answered me;
>   he delivered me from all my fears.
> Those who look to him are radiant;
>   their faces are never covered with
>   shame.
> This poor man called, and the LORD
>   heard him;
>   he saved him out of all his troubles.
> The angel of the LORD encamps around
>   those who fear him,
>   and he delivers them (Psalm 34:4–7).

How marvelous it is to serve the God who shows himself strong during our weakest moments! The Lord wants to use his "breakout" power to transform our times of fear and trouble into a birthing place for new mercies and grace. Every challenge we face is just

another opportunity to pray and yield ourselves to his tender hands. Then we can rest
in God and wait patiently for him to "break
out" against our enemies.

Dear Father, lead us step by step every
day of our lives. Give us a humble, childlike heart that will listen for and then obey
your voice. We want to experience your
power so that spiritual walls will be broken down in Christ's name. Arise, O Lord,
and let your enemies be scattered! We ask
this in the authority of Jesus' name.
Amen.

Fresh Faith
What Happens When Real Faith Ignites God's People
Jim Cymbala with Dean Merrill

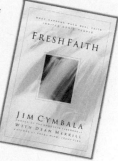

In an era laced with worry about the present and cynicism about the future, in a climate in which we've grown tired of hoping for miracles and wary of trumped-up claims that only disappoint, comes a confident reminder that God has not fallen asleep. He has not forgotten his people nor retreated into semi-retirement. On the contrary, he is ready to respond to real faith wherever he finds it.

Pastor Jim Cymbala insists that authentic, biblical faith is simple, honest, and utterly dependent upon God, a faith capable of transforming your life, your church, and the nation itself.

Jim Cymbala calls us back to the authentic, biblical faith—a fiery, passionate preoccupation with God that will restore our troubled children, our wounded marriages, and our broken and divided churches. Born out of the heart and soul of The Brooklyn Tabernacle, the message of *Fresh Faith* is illustrated by true stories of men and women whose lives have been changed through the power of faith.

Hardcover 0-310-23007-1
Audio Pages® Abridged Cassettes 0-310-23006-3
Audio Pages® Unabridged CD 0-310-23639-8

Pick up a copy today at your favorite bookstore!

GRAND RAPIDS, MICHIGAN 49530

FRESH POWER

Experiencing the Vast Resources of the Spirit of God

Jim Cymbala with Dean Merrill

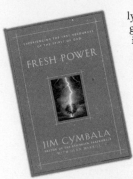

Pastor Jim Cymbala of The Brooklyn Tabernacle has taught his congregation how God's mighty power can infuse their present-day lives and the mission of their church. He continued that teaching nationally in his best-selling books *Fresh Wind, Fresh Fire* and *Fresh Faith*, which tell about the transforming power of God's love to convert prostitutes, addicts, the homeless, and people of all races and stations in life.

Now in *Fresh Power* Cymbala continues to spread the word about the power of God's Holy Spirit in the lives of those who seek him. Fresh power, Cymbala says, is available to us as we desire the Holy Spirit's constant infilling and learn what it means to be Spirit filled, both as individuals and as the church. With the book of Acts as the basis for his study, Cymbala shows how the daily lives of first-century Christians were defined by their belief in God's Word, in the constant infilling of his Spirit, and in the clear and direct responses of obedience to Scripture. He shows that that same life in Christ through the power of the Holy Spirit is available today for pastors, leaders, and laypeople who are longing for revival.

Hardcover 0-310-23008-X
Audio Pages® Abridged Cassettes 0-310-23467-X
Audio Pages® Unabridged CD 0-310-24200-2

Pick up a copy today at your favorite bookstore!

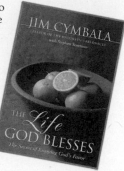

He's Been Faithful
Trusting God to Do What Only He Can Do
Carol Cymbala with Ann Spangler

Carol Cymbala's ministry in a tough inner-city neighborhood in New York can be summed up in one word: unlikely. She is the director and songwriter for a Grammy Award-winning choir—yet she doesn't read music. She is the pastor's wife in a 6,000-member congregation filled with people of color—and she is white. A shy girl who struggled to get through school, she is the last person you'd expect to stand before a packed house at Radio City Music Hall, confidently directing The Brooklyn Tabernacle Choir.

But Carol's God is the God of the unlikely. *He's Been Faithful* is an honest story about the struggles we all face and the power of God to help us. It is told through Carol's eyes as well as through the eyes of various members of The Brooklyn Tabernacle Choir who have experienced the grace of Christ in remarkable ways. *He's Been Faithful* tells the story of the way God works despite—or maybe because of—our many inadequacies.

But Carol's faith hasn't always come easily. There have been times of wavering and challenge, like the time a man walked down the aisle of the church pointing a gun at her husband, Jim. Or like the time she was assaulted outside the church. Or like the time she wanted to pack up her children and run away from the city for good because of what was happening to her family.

Whether you are a pastor, a choir director, or someone who is seeking a deeper experience of God, *He's Been Faithful* will renew your faith and increase your understanding that only Jesus can fill that deep, deep longing we all have for something more in life.

Hardcover 0-310-23652-5
Audio Pages® Abridged Cassettes 0-310-23668-1

GOD'S GRACE FROM GROUND ZERO
Seeking God's Heart for the Future of Our World
Jim Cymbala with Stephen Sorenson

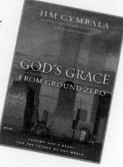

Out of the horror of September 11 emerges a startling message of hope. Pastor Jim Cymbala believes that in the face of unspeakable tragedy, God is reaching out to the heart of a grieving city, to the people of a wounded nation, and to a world that fears what the future may hold.

God's Grace from Ground Zero assures us that God hates the senseless evil that destroyed thousands of lives, and that this is a time when he is pouring out his mercy in a special way. The harvest is ripe, hearts that were closed are open to the gospel, and today, not tomorrow, is when we have the opportunity and responsibility to express Jesus through our words and through our deeds. Now is the time to love our families, our friends, and those around us. Now is the time to trust God and live for him as never before. And now, in the midst of our grief, our fear, and our lack of answers for things that make no sense, is the time to worship God with all our hearts.

We want to hear from you. Please send your
comments about this book to us in care of the
address below. Thank you.

GRAND RAPIDS, MICHIGAN 49530
www.zondervan.com